cool
names
FOR BABIES

ST. MARTIN'S GRIFFIN

NEW YORK

cool names
FOR BABIES

REVISED AND UPDATED

PAMELA REDMOND SATRAN
& LINDA ROSENKRANTZ

www.stmartins.com

Book design by Stephanie Huntwork

Library of Congress Cataloging-in-Publication Data

Satran, Pamela Redmond.
  Cool names for babies / Pamela Redmond Satran and Linda Rosenkrantz.—Rev. and updated, 1st ed.
    p. cm.
  Rev. ed. of: Cool names for babies. 2003
  Includes index.
  ISBN-13: 978-0-312-37786-1
  ISBN-10: 0-312-37786-X
  1. Names, Personal—Dictionaries. I. Rosenkrantz, Linda. II. Satran, Pamela Redmond. Cool names for babies. III. Title.

  CS2377.S2653 2008
  929.4′4—dc22   2007039730

20 19 18 17 16 15 14 13 12 11

contents

iii. pre-cool cool
OLD NAMES

iv. new cool
CREATIVE NAMES

introduction

What are the cool names for babies?

That's one of the first questions most parents and interviewers ask us. Which names are cool? And how can I choose a cool name for my child?

Cool has taken over from such qualities as tradition and stylishness as the premier criterion of a name. Even those parents who want to give their children family names or names with ethnic significance often want those choices to be cool.

In the five years since the first edition of *Cool Names for Babies* was published, the cool factor has become even more important in choosing a name. The Web, the explosion in cool-related pregnancy and baby paraphernalia of all kinds, the fascination with celebrity babies (and their cool names), and the general obsession with coolness all fuel the passion.

So what's new and exciting when it comes to cool names? And how *do* you choose a name for your child that's cool not just today but forever?

COOL MEANS UNUSUAL

The new cool names are almost all unusual. With once uncommon names like Madison and Ethan, Joshua and Sophia now in the Top 10, you have to move further and further from the mainstream to find a name that's truly distinctive and, yes, cool. While fashionable classic names such as Jack and Emma may still be wonderful choices (and perhaps ultimately the right ones for you), you can't really call them cool. And trendy names ranging from Aidan to Ava, Tyler to Taylor are simply too widely used to be considered really cool.

COOL IS DIVERSE

The first generation of cool names—Jodi and Jordan, Sunshine and Shane—were homogenous, designed to blur boundaries between genders, races, and nationalities. The new cool names, on the other hand, celebrate diversity by including names from around the world, ethnic choices that trumpet family heritage or move beyond it. Cool names include elaborately feminine names for girls, macho names for boys, and choices that play with gender stereotypes. There are names resurrected from ancient cultures as well as newly minted choices.

COOL GOES BEYOND CONVENTION

The pool of cool names draws from sources far beyond the traditional roster of first names, to include surnames, place names, nature and day names, and word names. And why stop there? In this book, we offer some new categories no one ever thought of before: foreign word names, for instance, like Vrai.

COOL DRAWS ON POPULAR CULTURE

The world is full of inspiration for cool baby naming—and more full every day, thanks to the cool names of characters in movies and books as well as the names of starbabies and celebrities. And by celebrities we don't mean just movie stars: Here you'll find lists of inspirational names of supermodels, athletes, rappers, artists, and writers, too.

DON'T BE AFRAID OF COOL

When we were growing up, if you had a name like Sonata or Samson, other kids thought you were weird. But now that the concept of cool permeates the culture, kids are more apt to admire distinctive names. Our own children's friends include an Ash and a Dash, a (boy) Robin and a (girl) Baldwin, a Miles and a Remi and a Lex and a Xan. So if the only thing that's stopping you from choosing a cooler name is worrying about how your child will handle it, don't let that deter you.

THERE'S MORE THAN ONE WAY TO BE COOL

Cool wouldn't be cool if it was too regimented. There are cool names to suit any sensibility or level of cool, from the hot—popular names such as Ella and Elijah that are widely considered cool—to the frankly far-out. How far you want to go depends on your taste, your sense of adventure, and where you live. One Manhattan-based parent we know, for instance, recently rejected the name Oscar as "too common"—though in most parts of the country, Oscar is still too cool for consideration.

So, what if you're one of those people who realize you don't want to go even halfway to Oscar? What if you read this book and find yourself intrigued, entertained, inspired . . . but in the end a lot more convinced than you realized that you want to give your child a plain, solid, and decidedly uncool name like John or Elizabeth?

So what indeed. A name is not your personal style statement, a choice with which to impress the world. Rather, you should think of it as something that will identify your child for the rest of his life, a label she will have to live with forever. You may decide that cool is a desirable component of such a lifelong imprimatur. But then again, you may decide that, when it comes to a name, you want nothing to do with cool (just know you'll probably have to suffer the consequences when your child is a teenager).

Whether or not you end up with a cool name, you owe it to your baby and your choice of a name to read this book. For one thing, we offer hundreds and hundreds of naming options here that you won't find anywhere else. We'll open your eyes to a way of thinking about names that no other book, no other source can. And you'll know for certain, after reading this book, what makes for a cool name—even if you decide that un-cool is cool enough for you.

hot cool

MAINSTREAM NAMES

isabella

TOP 100 OF COOL

Many of the names commonly thought of as cool are in fact widely used. With Ava at number 5 on the girls' popularity list—there were nearly seventeen thousand Avas born in the most recent year counted—such once offbeat choices as Addison and Ashton can't be far behind. Here, we go down the most recent list of the 1,000 Most Popular Names from the Social Security Office and rank the top cool names among them.

Depending on your personal tolerance for cool, you may see the names here as either outrageous or a big yawn. In either case, for first-time parents this list may be an eye-opening look at just how popular these choices are. To give you a real-numbers idea of volume, there were more than twenty-one thousand boys named Aidan or Aiden (we didn't even count the Aydens, etc.) born in one recent year—that's more than four hundred in every state. And for those who want to find a name that's cool without being unique or unusual or wild, these can offer a good compromise.

A word on our methods: Noted here is each name's standing

on our Cool Top 100, as well as, in parentheses, its rank on the most recent conventional popularity list. And while cool is a subjective quality, prompting many differences of opinion even between the two of us, for the most part we excluded classic names such as Michael and Elizabeth, as well as older, perhaps once cool but now overexposed favorites like Joshua and Madison. Any parent who wants to search the national list of top baby names, and make his or her own decisions about which are cool, can find the top 1,000 online at *http://www.ssa.gov/OACT/babynames*.

girls

1. ISABELLA (4)
2. AVA (5)
3. OLIVIA (7)
4. SOPHIA (9)
5. MIA (13)
6. GRACE (17)
7. CHLOE (18)
8. ELLA (21)
9. ADDISON (27)
10. SAVANNAH (30)
11. LILY (33)
12. ALEXA (39)
13. NEVAEH (43)
14. GABRIELLA (50)
15. AVERY (52)
16. ZOE (54)
17. RILEY (55)
18. MAYA (57)
19. BROOKLYN (67)
20. AUDREY (68)
21. MADELINE (71)
22. JOCELYN (73)
23. PAIGE (76)
24. ARIANNA/ARIANA (77, 78)
25. MARIAH (81)
26. AMELIA (82)
27. AALIYAH (91)
28. AUBREY (92)
29. NATALIA (94)
30. GIANNA (98)
31. JAYLA (99)
32. LAYLA (100)
33. MYA (101)
34. GRACIE (103)

35. ADRIANA (106)

36. KEIRA (109)

37. BAILEY (112)

38. EVA (124)

39. SOPHIE (125)

40. SERENITY (135)

41. RUBY (137)

42. MIRANDA (139)

43. ASHLYN (141)

44. DAISY (149)

45. SUMMER (154)

46. SADIE (157)

47. REESE (159)

48. ALEXIA (164)

49. ELLIE (175)

50. SIENNA (177)

51. BELLA (181)

52. NADIA (188)

53. JULIANNA (194)

54. KYRA (195)

55. HOPE (200)

56. ANGELICA (208)

57. CIARA (213)

58. CADENCE (214)

59. McKENNA (217)

60. CASSANDRA (219)

61. JOSEPHINE (223)

62. STELLA (241)

63. BETHANY (244)

64. NORA (245)

65. PIPER (246)

66. TESSA (252)

67. HEAVEN (253)

68. VIOLET (261)

69. CECILIA (265)

70. MACY (267)

71. GEORGIA (273)

72. LOLA (280)

73. CAROLINA (281)

74. TATIANA (283)

75. SELENA (285)

76. JOSIE (291)

77. SCARLETT (297)

78. EMERSON (305)

79. EDEN (320)

80. ELIZA (325)

81. LILA (329)

82. ASIA (332)

83. FIONA (333)

84. IVY (334)

85. PRESLEY (348)

86. TATUM (349)

87. SAMARA (351)

88. LONDON (353)

89. NATASHA (357)

90. TALIA (363)

91. ALICE (383)

92. HARLEY (388)

93. SERENA (396)

94. ANYA (405)

95. MARLEY (415)

96. HAYDEN (416)

97. SAGE (417)

98. ELLE (480)

99. LUNA (516)

100. WILLOW (529)

boys

1. ETHAN (4)

2. NOAH (15)

3. LOGAN (19)

4. CHRISTIAN (21)

5. NATHAN (23)

6. ELIJAH (29)

7. AIDEN (30)—

combined with AIDAN

spelling, would be #4 on

Social Security list

8. ANGEL (31)

9. CALEB (34)

10. JACK (35)

11. JACKSON (36)

12. MASON (39)

13. ISAIAH (40)

14. EVAN (42)

15. ISAAC (48)

16. JAYDON (50)

17. CONNOR (53)

18. HUNTER (54)

19. OWEN (58)

20. LUCAS (59)

21. ADRIAN (63)

22. JULIAN (65)

23. JEREMIAH (71)

24. CARTER (75)

25. SEBASTIAN (76)

26. IAN (81)

27. WYATT (82)

28. CHASE (83)

29. COLE (84)

30. DOMINIC (85)

31. TRISTAN (86)

32. CARSON (87)

33. LIAM (98)

34. RILEY (101)

35. BRADY (105)

36. PATRICK (110)

37. COLIN (111)

38. MARCUS (112)

39. COOPER (113)

40. PRESTON (114)

41. JOSIAH (117)

42. OSCAR (118)

43. ASHTON (121)

44. COLTON (133)

45. LEVI (135)

46. DAMIAN (136)

47. ELI (139)

48. NOLAN (145)

49. GIOVANNI (146)

50. BRODY (147)

51. MICAH (148)

52. MALACHI (150)

53. GEORGE (153)

54. OLIVER (173)

55. LEONARDO (184)

56. ELIAS (186)

57. TRENTON (192)

58. DONOVAN (198)

59. MILES (202)

60. DREW (205)

61. AVERY (212)

62. MADDOX (235)

63. LEO (236)

64. ZANE (243)

65. SAWYER (247)

66. HUDSON (249)

67. ASHER (252)

68. GRIFFIN (254)

69. RYDER (257)

70. MACY (267)

71. ZION (266)

72. EZEKIEL (269)

73. CHANCE (273)

74. MATEO (274)

75. XANDER (278)

76. JOAQUIN (286)

77. CADE (288)

78. LINCOLN (300)

79. JUDE (330)

80. CHARLIE (337)

81. LELAND (342)

82. LUCA (349)

83. ORLANDO (356)

84. DECLAN (364)

85. MAXIMUS (374)

86. HOLDEN (384)

87. JUSTICE (411)

88. ROWAN (427)

89. MOSES (445)

90. FINN (456)

91. DESMOND (464)

92. ROCCO (490)

93. CRUZ (500)

94. ORION (529)

95. JASPER (568)

96. ROMEO (574)

97. AUGUST (618)

98. MILO (679)

99. ENZO (737)

100. MATTHIAS (813)

molly polly poppy

COOLATOR

Often, it doesn't take much to change the cool status of a name. For many girls' names, all you have to do is add an *a* to the end to bump them up several coolness levels: Natalie to Natalia, Susan to Susanna—you get the picture. The point is that with a bit of ingenuity you can ramp up a name you like to a similar one that's cooler, or tone it down if you want to go in a quieter direction. Here are some examples:

girls

UNCOOL	COOL	COOLER
ANNE	ANNA	ANNIKA
AVIS	AVA	AVERY
BRIANNA	BRYN	BRONTE
CAROL	CAROLINE	CAROLINA
CASEY	CASSIDY	CASSANDRA
CHARLENE	CHARLOTTE	CHIARA
CINDY	SYDNEY	SIDONY

CRYSTAL	JADE	RUBY
DAWN	AURORA	ZORA
DIANE	DIANA	DINAH
DORA	NORA	ISADORA
FLORIDA	SAVANNAH	MEMPHIS
GENA	GENEVIEVE	GENEVA
GEORGETTE	GEORGIA	GEORGINA
GWEN	GWYNNE	GWYNETH
HEATHER	DAISY	VIOLET
IVANA	IVORY	IVY
JAMIE	JAMES	JAMAICA
JAN	JANNA	JANE
JEANETTE	JENNA	GEMMA
JOAN	JUNE	JUNO
JOANNE	JOANNA	JOSIE
JULIE	JULIA	JULIET
LILIAN	LILY	LILO
LISA	LIZA	ELIZA
LORI	LAURA	LAURENCE
LUCILLE	LUCY	LUCIA
MARIE	MARIA	MIREILLE
MERRY	MERCY	MERCEDES
MOLLY	POLLY	POPPY
PATTY	PATRICIA	PATIENCE
ROSEMARY	SAGE	SAFFRON
SAMANTHA	SAMARA	SAM
SELMA	SELENA	SERENA
SHYANNE	CHEYENNE	SHILOH

UNCOOL	COOL	COOLER
STACY	LACEY	GRACIE
STEPHANIE	STELLA	STORY
TAMMY	TAMARA	TAMAR
WILMA	WILLOW	WILLA
ZENA	ZEN	ZENOBIA

boys

UNCOOL	COOL	COOLER
ADOLPH	ADRIAN	ADLAI
ARNOLD	ARNE	ARNO
ARTHUR	ARCHER	ARTEMAS
ASHLEY	ASHER	ASH
BILL	WILL	WILLEM
BRUCE	BRYCE	BRUNO
CHUCK	CHARLIE	CARLOS
CRAIG	CRISPIN	CRUZ
DARRYL	DARIUS	DASHIELL
DENNIS	DENNISON	DENVER
EDDIE	EDWARD	NED
HANK	HENRY	ENZO
IVAN	IVOR	IVO
JEFF	JEB	JEX
JIMMY	JAMES	JAMESON
JOHN	JACK	GIACOMO
KEN	BEN	SVEN

KENNETH	KENYON	CANYON
LEE	LEO	LEONARDO
MANNY	EMANUEL	EMMETT
MIKE	MAC	MAGUIRE
MILTON	MILES	MILO
MONROE	TYLER	TRUMAN
MONTY	MONTANA	MONTEZ
MORRIS	MORRISON	MORRISEY
RAYMOND	RAY	RAOUL
RONALD	ROONEY	RONAN
SCOTT	SCHUYLER	SCOUT
WAYNE	KANE	ZANE
WILFRED	WILLIAM	WILLEM

COOLEST
FLOWER NAME
• • •
Poppy

isla

BRITISH NAMES

Let's face it, our baby-naming contemporaries across the Atlantic are often a step or two ahead of us. This means that some of the hottest names in Great Britain, Scotland, Ireland, and Wales are still cool—and underused—choices over here, as seen below. The asterisk indicates a name currently in the Top 100 in one or more of the British Isles.

girls

AILSA	BRIONY/BRYONY	EMER*
AISLING*	CATRIONA	EUGENIE
ALICE*	CERYS*	EVA*
AMELIE*	CLEMENTINE	EVIE*
ANNABEL	CLOVER	FLORA
ANWEN	CRESSIDA	FREYA*
AOIFE	DAISY*	GEORGINA
ARABELLA	DEMI*	GRACIE*
ARAMINTA	EILIDH*	GRANIA
BEATRIX	ELLIE*	HERMIONE

HONORA

IMOGEN*

IONA*

IRIS

ISLA*

JEMIMA

JOCASTA

LAYLA*

LETTICE

LIBBY*

LYDIA*

MAEVE*

MAISIE*

MATILDA*

MILLIE*

NEVE*

NIAMH*

NICOLA

ORLA*

PHILIPPA

PIPPA

POPPY*

RHIANNON

RHONWEN

ROISIN*

ROSIE*

RUBY*

SINEAD*

SIOBHAN

SORCHA

TAMSIN

TILLY*

UNA/OONA

ZARA*

boys

ALFIE*

ANGUS*

ARCHIE*

ARRAN*

AUGUSTINE

BALTHAZAR

BARNABY

BILLY*

CALLUM/CALUM*

CIARAN*

CILLIAN*

COLM*

CORMAC*

CRISPIN

DARRAGH*

DECLAN*

DUNCAN

EAMON

ELLIS*

EUAN/EWAN

FELIX

FERGUS

FINLAY/
 FINLEY*

FINN*

GREGOR*

HAMISH*

HARRY*

HARVEY*

HUGH*

INIGO

JASPER

JAY*

KAI*

KENZIE*

KIAN*

KIERAN*

KILLIAN

LACHLAN

LAIRD

LENNON*

LEO*

LEON*

LEWIS*/
 LOUIS

LORCAN

LUCA*

MALACHY

NIALL*	REECE*/RHYS*	RORY*
OSCAR*	REX	RUPERT
PIERS	ROHAN/ROWAN	SEAMUS
REDMOND	RONAN*	TARQUIN

COOLEST
IRISH PLACE NAME
• • •
Galway

cruz

INTERNATIONAL NAMES

This is one of the hottest and coolest categories of baby names today, with much mixing and matching of ethnicities—it's not at all unusual to find a Paloma O'Hennessey, for instance, or a Connor Cohen, or a Mischa Brown. The vast range of possible choices puts it beyond the reach of this book: For further selections, you can check our *Baby Name Bible,* as well as *Beyond Jennifer & Jason, Madison & Montana,* or search the Web for name sites overseas (try to find the real ones, not some American listing of Italian or French names—they are often incomplete and don't include the really interesting foreign choices). There are also a lot of international names sprinkled throughout this book. The select group below consists of those that we think are especially appealing and, yes, cool.

girls

ALEJANDRA	AMAIA
ALESSIA	AMÉLIE
ALEXANE	ANIKA

ANJA	FIA
ANOUSH	FINULA
ANTONELLA	FIORELLA
AZIZA	FLEUR
BEATRIZ	FRANCESCA
BENICIA	FYODORA
CALANDRA	GEMMA
CALLA	GIANNA
CARMEN	GIOIA
CHIARA	GUADALUPE
CLEA	IMAN
CLEMENCE	INEZ
COSIMA	INGRID
DAGNY	IRINA
DAMIANA	IZARA
DANICA	JAMILA
DELPHINE	JANICA
EBBA	JOCASTA
EDWIGE	KALILA
ELETTRA	KALINDI
ELIANA	KATYA
ELODIE	LAILA/LAYLA
ESTRELLA	LARISA
EUGENIE	LAURENZA
FABIENNE	LIA
FEDERICA	LILOU
FEODORA	LIVIA
FERNANDA	LUCIANA

LUCIENNE

LUIZA

LUZ

MALIA

MANON

MARINE

MARISOL

MARIT

MELANTHA

MERCEDES

MIGNON

NADYA

NATALYA

NIAMH

NOEMI

OCÉANE

ODILE

ONDINE

ORIANA

OTTALINE

OTTAVIA

PALOMA

PAOLINA

PAZ

PIA

PILAR

QUINTANA/QUINTINA

RAFFAELA/RAPHAELA

RAQUEL

SANDRINE

SANNE

SARITA

SASKIA

SAVITA

SEVERINE

SIDONIE

SIGNY

SIMONE

SOLANGE

SOLEDAD

SYLVIE/SILVIE

TAMAR

TATIANA

VALENTINA

VENEZIA

VIOLETTA

VIVECA

XANTHE

ZUZANNA

boys

ADRIANO

AKIM

ALESSIO

ALEXEI

ALVARO

AMEDEO	GWILYM
ANDREAS	HELIO
ANGUS	ILYA
ARA	IVAR
ARAM	IVO
ARI	JANOS
ARJUN	JOAQUIN
ARMANDO	KAI
AURELIO	KEES
BAPTISTE	KRISTOF
BJORN	LARS
CILLIAN	LAURENT
CORMAC	LEIF/LIEF
COSMO	LEV
CRUZ	LORENZO/RENZO/ENZO
DIDIER	LUC
DIMITRI	LUCIANO
DION	LUCIEN
DJANGO	MARCEAU
ELIO	MATEO/MATTEO
ÉTIENNE	MIGUEL
FABIANO	MIKHAIL
FABRIZIO	MILOS
FRITZ	MISHA
FYODOR	NAVARRO
GASTON	NICASIO
GUILLAUME	NIKO
GUNNAR	NIKOS

ODIN	SVEN
OHAN	TADEO/TADDEO
OLIVIER	TAJ
ORI	TANGUY
ORION	THIBAULT
ORLANDO	THIERRY
PABLO	TIBOR
PADRAIG	TOMASZ
PAOLO	TORQUIL
PASCAL	UMBERTO
PIET	VASILI
RAFIQ	WILLEM
RAOUL	WOLF
REMI	ZENO
ROMAN	ZEUS
SOREN	ZEVI
STELLEN	ZIV

COOLEST
ROYAL NAME

• • •

Beatrix

leevi

WHAT EUROPEANS CALL COOL

What are the top names actually chosen by Continental parents these days? Here are the most recently available Top 10 lists from four of the most influential countries: France, Italy, Spain, and Germany—they include a few really surprising choices: Leon? Nerea?

FRANCE

girls	boys
1. EMMA	ENZO
2. LÉA	MATHIS
3. MANON	LUCAS
4. CLARA	HUGO
5. CHLOÉ	MATHÉO
6. INÈS	NATHAN
7. CAMILLE	THÉO
8. SARAH	NOAH
9. OCÉANE	MATTÉO
10. JADE	THOMAS

ITALY

girls	boys
1. GIULIA	ANDREA
2. ALESSIA	LORENZO
3. ALICE	SIMONE
4. CHIARA	PAOLO
5. GAIA	MARCO
6. GINEVRA	FRANCESCO
7. EMMA	LUCA
8. ILARIA	TOMASSO
9. VIOLA	CHRISTIAN
10. LUDOVICA	ALESSANDRO

SPAIN

girls	boys
1. LUCIA	ALEJANDRO
2. MARIA	DAVID
3. PAULA	DANIEL
4. LAURA	PABLO
5. MARTA	ADRIAN
6. ALBA	ALVARO
7. ANDREA	JAVIER
8. CLAUDIA	SERGIO
9. SARA	CARLOS
10. NEREA	MARCOS

GERMANY

girls	boys
1. MARIE	LEON
2. SOPHIE/SOFIE	MAXIMILIAN
3. MARIA	ALEXANDER
4. ANNA/ANNE	LUKAS/LUCAS
5. LEONIE	PAUL
6. LENA	LUCA
7. EMILY	TIM
8. JOHANNA	FELIX
9. LAURA	DAVID
10. LEA/LEAH	ELIAS

And from several other countries abroad, here are some more unusual recent Top 10 options:

girls

AADA (Finland)	IIDA (Finland)
ADELA (Czech Republic)	IRIS (The Netherlands)
ALVA (Sweden)	IZARO (Basque Country)
ANOUK (The Netherlands)	JAVIERA (Chile)
BEATRIZ (Brazil)	LÉA (Belgium)
CATALINA (Chile)	LENA (Austria)
CONSTANZA (Chile)	LEONIE (Austria,
ELISKA (Czech Republic)	Switzerland)
FERNANDA (Chile)	LETICIA (Brazil)
FREJA (Denmark)	LINNÉA (Sweden)
IDA (Norway, Denmark)	MAJA (Sweden)

MALIN (Norway)

MANON (Belgium)

NAROA (Basque Country)

PETRA (Hungary)

RÉKA (Hungary)

SANNE (The Netherlands)

TELMA (Iceland)

TEREZA (Czech Republic)

THEA (Norway)

ZSÓFIA (Hungary)

boys

ANDREAS (Norway)

ANTERO (Finland)

CRISTOBAL (Chile)

DAAN (The Netherlands)

EETU (Finland)

FABIAN (Austria)

FILIP (Sweden)

FLORIAN (Austria)

HUGO (Sweden)

JOÃO (Portugal)

LEEVI (Finland)

LUCA (Switzerland)

MADS (Denmark)

MAGNUS (Norway, Denmark)

MATEJ (Czech Republic)

MIKKEL (Denmark)

MILAN (Belgium)

OSCAR (Sweden)

ROBBE (Belgium)

SEM (The Netherlands)

STANISLAW (Poland)

TAMPANI (Finland)

TIAGO (Portugal)

VEETI (Finland)

anna anya anina

THE EXOTICIZER

If you like the idea of an international name, another approach is to take a traditional name and exoticize it—a perfect way to honor a grandparent or other ancestor by using a more unusual and exotic version of his or her name. The examples below show how to do this in two steps, going from classic to cooler to coolest.

CLASSIC	MORE EXOTIC	MOST EXOTIC
ALEXANDER	ALESSANDRO	ALESSIO
ANDREW	ANDRÉ	ANDREAS
ANNA	ANYA	ANINA
CHRISTOPHER	KRISTOF	CHRISTO
CLAIRE	CLARISSA	CHIARA
ELIZABETH	ELSBETH	ELIZABETTA
ELLEN	ELENA	ELEONARA
EMILY	AMELIE	AMALYA
FIONA	FINULA	FIONNUALA
FRANCIS	FRANCISCO	CISCO

GABRIELLA	GABI	GAVI
GRACE	GRAZIA	ENGRACIA
HANNAH	JANNA	ZANNA
ISABEL	ISABELLA	ISABEAU
JANE	JOHANNA	SINEAD
JULIAN	JULIO	GIULIO
KAYLIE	KALILA	KALINDI
KERRY	KERRIS	KERENSA
LAURENCE	LORENZO	LARS
LUCY	LUCIA	LUZ
MARC	MARCO	MARCELLO
MATTHEW	MATTHIAS	MATTEO
MICHAEL	MIKHAIL	MIKKO
NICHOLAS	NICO	NICOLAI
NINA	NIA	NIAMH
PAUL	PAOLO	PAVLO
PETER	PIERO	PIET
PHILIPPA	PIPPA	PIPPI
ROLAND	ORLANDO	ROLLO
SARA	ZARA	ZAHARA
SOPHIA	SOFIA	ZOFIA
STEPHEN	STEFANO	ESTEBAN
SUSANNA	ZUZANNA	ZUZU
SYDNEY	SIDONIE	SIDONIA
THEODORA	TEODORA	FEODORA
THOMAS	TOMAS	TOMASSO
WILLIAM	WILLEM	GWYLYM

bolivia

PLACE NAMES

As a category, place names have been so well visited over the past couple of decades that many selections from this group are no longer distinctive enough to be considered truly cool. However, some individual place names do retain a fresh feeling and so still merit the official Seal of Coolness. For the most part, these are the more unusual choices as well as the more exotic places—or kinds of places, which include rivers and national parks. However, a few old favorites—India stands out—are as cool as they ever were. Some place names can be used for boys, but most now veer toward the feminine side.

ABILENE	ANDORRA	ASSISI
ADELAIDE	AQUITAINE	ATLANTA
AFRICA	ARABIA	AUSTRIA
ALABAMA	ARAGON	AVALON
ALAMO	ARGENTINA	BAJA
ALBANY	ASPEN	BERLIN

BIMINI	DUBLIN	MAJORCA
BOLIVIA	ELBA	MALTA
BOSTON	ENGLAND	MANILA
BRASILIA	EVEREST	MARBELLA
BRAZIL	GALWAY	MEMPHIS
BRISTOL	GENOA	MIAMI
CADIZ	GLASGOW	MILAN
CAIRO	GUERNSEY	MOROCCO
CALAIS	HARLEM	NAIROBI
CALEDONIA	HAVANA	NEVIS
CAMDEN	HOLLAND	NILE
CASPIAN	HUDSON	ODESSA
CATALINA	IBERIA	OLYMPIA
CATHAY	INDIA	OSLO
CAYMAN	INDIO	PALERMO
CEYLON	IRELAND	PALMA
CHARLESTON	ITALIA	PANAMA
CLUNY	JAKARTA	PERSIA
COLOMBIA	JAMAICA	PERU
CORSICA	JAVA	PHILIPPINE
CUBA	JERSEY	PORTLAND
CYPRUS	KENYA	QUEBEC
DANUBE	KINGSTON	QUINTANA
DELPHI	KYOTO	QUITO
DENVER	LONDON	RALEIGH
DOMINICA	LOUISIANA	RENO
DONEGAL	LOURDES	RIO
DOVER	LUCCA	ROMA

ROMANY	SICILY	TRINIDAD
RUSSIA	SIENA	UMBRIA
SAHARA	SONOMA	VALENCIA
SALEM	SONORA	VENICE
SAMARA	SYDNEY	VERONA
SAMOA	TAHITI	VIENNA
SANTIAGO	TANGIER	YORK
SENEGAL	TIVOLI	
SEVILLA	TRENTON	

COOLEST
STATE CAPITAL
NAME

. . .

Atlanta

venus & violet

BAD GIRL/GOOD GIRL NAMES

It may be difficult for people on the brink of parenthood to admit this, but it's cool to be bad. It was cool when you were younger . . . and it's still going to be cool when your baby-to-be is a lot, lot older. And in this age of extremes, it's also cool to be good. Prime example: Madonna, whose own name makes both the lists, gave her daughter the saintly name of Lourdes, the place where the Virgin Mary miraculously heals the sick, but calls her by the sultry nickname Lola. For further illustrations of the bad girl/good girl concept and more name ideas for your own angelic hellion, consult the following list.

bad girls

APHRODITE	COCO
ASIA	DELILAH
BATHSHEBA	DESDEMONA
BLAZE	DESIREE
CAYENNE	DIVA
CLEO	DIXIE

DOMINIQUE	SADIE
EGYPT	SALOME
FANNY	SCARLETT
FIFI	SHEBA
FLAME	STORM
GIGI	TALLULAH
JAZZ	TEMPEST
JEZEBEL	TRIXIE
JINX	VENUS
LANA	XENA
LILITH	YASMINE
LOLA	YOLANDA
LOLITA	ZULEIKA
LULU	
MABEL	good girls
MADONNA	ABIGAIL
MAMIE	AGNES
MEDEA	ALICE
MITZI	ALLEGRA
MONIQUE	AMITY
MOXIE	AMY
PANDORA	ANGEL
PEACHES	ANGELICA
QUEENIE	ANNA
RAVEN	ARIEL
RIPLEY	CARA
ROXY	CATHERINE
RUBY	CELIA

CHARITY	LOURDES
CHARLOTTE	LUCY
CHASTITY	MADONNA (yes, both)
CLAIRE	MARGARET
CLARA	MARIAN
COMFORT	MARTHA
CONSTANCE	MERCY
ELEANOR	MIRIAM
ESTHER	MODESTY
FAITH	NAOMI
FELICITY	NORA
FLEUR	OLIVE
FLORA	PATIENCE
FRANCES	PEARL
GRACE	PIPER
HELEN	POLLY
HELENA	POSEY
HONOR	PRIMROSE
HOPE	PRISCILLA
JANE	PRUDENCE
JUDITH	RACHEL
JULIA	REBECCA
LACEY	ROSE
LAURA	ROSEMARY
LAUREL	RUTH
LILAC	SUNDAY
LILY	TEMPERANCE
LOUISA	TILLIE

TRUE   VIRGINIA
UNITY   WILLA
VERITY   WILLOW
VIOLET

COOLEST
SOUTHERN BELLE
NAME
• • •
Tallulah

macrae

MAC NAMES

In the past few years, we've heard of a lot of Mackenzies, McKennas, and McKaylas—in a wide array of spellings. Cute, maybe, but what's cool now are *Mac* names that go beyond these overpopular choices. And coolest of all are the *Mac*s you can lay genuine claim to from your family tree. Of course, creativity is allowed: You can honor an ancestor by putting the *Mac* prefix (which signifies "son of") before his first name, so grandpa Arthur inspires baby Macarthur.

It's commonly believed that *Mac* is Scottish and *Mc* is Irish, but in fact *Mc* is just a shortened form of *Mac*, and the two versions are found in both countries. Before a vowel, *Mac/Mc* was sometimes changes to *Mag*, as in Magee. With more than 1,600 *Mac/Mc* surnames in Ireland alone—and even more when you count spelling variations—there are too many wonderful choices to list here. A sampling of the best, good for girls as well as boys, follows; feel free to switch the *Mac*s and *Mc*s, the capitalization, and the spelling depending on your own family name and your taste. McCormac might just as easily, for example, be Macormick.

MACALLISTER	McCONNAL
MacARTHUR	McCORMAC
MACAULEY	McCOY
MacCARTER	McDERMOTT
MacDONALD	McDONNELL
MACKAY	McDOUGAL
MACLAREN	McDUFF
MACLEAN	McEWAN
MACMILLAN	McGEORGE
MACRAE	McGREGOR
MAGEE	McKINLEY
MAGUIRE	McLAUGHLIN
McADAM	McLEOD
McCABE	McNEILL
McCALLUM	McPHERSON
McCAREY	McRORY
McCARTHY	McTAVISH

orion

A, E, I, AND ESPECIALLY O VOWEL NAMES

One of the strongest baby-naming trends right now is names starting with one of the first four vowels. Six of the Top 10 girls' names on the current list start with a vowel, with many more following close behind. Names that begin or end with the letter *o* have long been particularly cool—we said this in our very first baby-naming book, *Beyond Jennifer & Jason,* and we say it still: The *O* names remain unsullied, appealing choices all, especially (though there are a few feminine selections) for boys. The options, of course, range far beyond those offered here, especially considering the entire world of Latinate names out there, but this group should give you a pretty good start.

THE O'S

ALDO	AMEDEO
ALEJANDRO	ANTONIO
ALESSANDRO	APOLLO
ALONZO	ARLO

ARMANDO	ELIO
ARNO	ELMO
AUGUSTO	EMILIO
AURELIO	ENZO
BENICIO/BENECIO	FABIO
BENNO	FERNANDO
BO	FRISCO
BRUNO	GIACOMO
CAIO	GIORGIO
CAIRO	HORATIO
CALICO	HUGO
CALIXTO	INDIGO
CALYPSO	INDIO
CAMEO	INIGO
CARLO	ITALO
CATO	IVO
CAYO	JERICHO
CICERO	JETHRO
CLAUDIO	LAREDO
CLEO	LEANDRO
CONSUELO	LEO
COSMO	LEONARDO
DANILO	LIDO
DARIO	LORENZO
DIEGO	LUCIANO
DJANGO	MARCO
DURANGO	MARINO
ECHO	MASSIMO

MATEO

MILO

MONTEGO

MOROCCO

NAVARRO

NEMO

NICO

NICOLO

NILO

O'BRIAN/O'BRIEN

O'CALLAHAN

O'CASEY

O'CONNOR

O'DONNELL

O'DONOVAN

O'FALLON

O'GRADY

O'HARA

O'KEEFE

O'NEAL/O'NEILL

O'REILLY

O'SHEA

O'SULLIVAN

OAK

OBADIAH

OBERON

OCEAN

OCEANA

OCTAVIA

OCTAVIO

ODELIA

ODESSA

ODETTE

ODILE

ODIN

ODION

OLAF

OLGA

OLIVE

OLIVER

OLIVIA

OLIVIER

OLWEN

OLYMPIA

OMAR

OONA

OPHELIA

ORCHID

OREN

ORIANA

ORION

ORLA

ORLANDO

ORSINO

ORSON

OSCAR

OTIS	RENO
OTTILIE	REO
OTTO	RIO
OWEN	ROCCO
OZ	RODRIGO
OZIAS	ROLLO
OZZIE	SCORPIO
PABLO	SERGIO
PAOLO	STEFANO
PEDRO	TADDEO
PHILO	THEO
PIERO	VIGGO
PLACIDO	VITTORIO
PLATO	WALDO
PRIMO	ZENO

THE *A*, *E*, AND *I*'S

While *O* names are the coolest of the bunch, names that start with other vowels are cool right now, too. Here's a selection for each gender, though some can be used for both girls and boys:

girls

ABBOTT	ADRIANA	AMAYA
ACACIA	AGATHA	AMELIA
ADA	AINSLEY	AMORY
ADAIR	ALCOTT	ANAÏS
ADDISON	ALICE	ANASTASIA
ADELAIDE	ALLEGRA	ANGELICA
ADELINE	AMARA	ANGELINA

ANNABEL	ELIORA	ISABEL
ANNIKA	ELIZA	ISABELLA
ANTONIA	ELLA	ISADORA
ANWEN	ELLE	ISLA
ANYA	ELLERY	IVY
ARA	ELLIOT	
ARABELLA	ELODIE	boys
ARAMINTA	EMERSON	AARON
ARDEN	EMERY	ABEL
ARIA	EMILIA	ABNER
ARIANA	ENGRACIA	ABRAHAM
ARWEN	ESMÉ	ACE
ASH	ESTHER	ADLAI
ASPEN	EUGENIA	ADRIAN
ATLANTA	EULALIA	ADRIANO
AUBREY	EVA	AIDAN
AUDEN	EVANGELINE	ALFIE
AUDREY	EVE	AMEDEO
AUGUST	IANTHE	AMIAS
AURORA	ILANA	AMOS
AVA	IMANI	ANDERSON
AVERY	IMARA	ANGUS
EDEN	IMOGEN	ARI
EDIE	INDIA	ARJUN
EDITH	INEZ	ASA
ELECTRA	INGRID	ASH
ELENA	IONE	ASHER
ELIANA	IRIS	ASHTON

ATTICUS	ELLERY	IAN
AUDEN	EMMETT	IKE
AUGUST	ENZO	ILYA
AUGUSTUS	EPHRAIM	ISAAC
EAMON	ESAU	ISAIAH
EBEN	ETHAN	ISAIAS
EDISON	EUAN/EWAN	IVAN
ELI	EVAN	IVAR
ELIAS	EZIO	
ELIJAH	EZRA	

COOLEST PALINDROME NAME

• • •

Elle

jasper

NEO-YUPPIE COOL NAMES

There is a certain kind of name that is considered cool by that segment of the upwardly mobile yet politically correct population we might call neo-yuppies. Neo-yuppies—the newest version of '80s yuppies and '90s bobos—like distinctive things but abhor ostentation; they have good taste but disdain convention; they appreciate the classics but prefer them with a modern twist. The names they like are to the left of the most popular list but far to the right of most choices in this book. You'll see them on the rosters of upscale nursery schools and hear them in the playgrounds of affluent neighborhoods, and you may like them yourself. And why not? They're good names, classic as well as cool, embodying style along with history. The only problem is that you may hear them far more than you want to in the years to come.

girls

ADDISON	ALICE
ALEXA	ALLEGRA

AMELIA	EMMA
ANNA	EVA
ANNABEL	EVE
ARABELLA	FAITH
ARDEN	FELICITY
AUDREY	FIONA
AVA	FLORA
BEATRICE	FRANCES
BEATRIX	FRANCESCA
BELLA	GABRIELLA
BROOKE	GEMMA
CARA	GEORGIA
CAROLINA	GRACE
CAROLINE	HELEN
CELIA	HELENA
CHARLOTTE	HOPE
CHLOE	INDIA
CLAIRE	IRIS
CLARA	ISABEL
CLARISSA	IVY
CLEMENTINE	JOSEPHINE
DAISY	JOSIE
DOROTHEA	JULIA
EDITH	JULIANA
ELEANOR	JULIET
ELIZA	KATE
ELLA	KITTY
ELLIE	LAURA

LEILA	SOPHIE
LILA	STELLA
LILY	SUSANNAH
LOUISA	TESS
LUCY	TESSA
MABEL	THEA
MADELEINE/	THEODORA
MADELINE	VIOLET
MAISIE	WILLA
MARGARET	ZOE
MAUDE	
MAYA	boys
MIRANDA	AIDAN
NATALIE	ALASTAIR
NELL	ANDERSON
NORA	ANDREW
OLIVIA	ASHER
PAIGE	BARNABY
PIPER	CALEB
POLLY	CALVIN
POPPY	CHARLIE
ROSE	CHRISTIAN
RUBY	CLAY
SADIE	COLE
SASHA	COLIN
SAWYER	DASHIELL
SLOANE	DOMINIC
SOPHIA	DUNCAN

43

ELI	JOE
ELIAS	JONAH
ELIJAH	JONAS
EMMETT	JULIAN
EZRA	LEO
FELIX	LEVI
FINN	LEWIS
FORREST	LIAM
FRANCIS	LUCAS
FREDERICK	LUKE
GABRIEL	MALCOLM
GEORGE	MAX
GRAHAM	MILES
GREGORY	MILO
GUS	NATHAN
HARRISON	NATHANIEL
HARRY	NED
HAYDEN	NICHOLAS
HENRY	NOAH
HUDSON	OLIVER
HUGH	ORSON
HUNTER	OSCAR
IKE	OWEN
ISAAC	PATRICK
ISAIAH	PHILIP
JACK	QUENTIN
JACKSON	QUINN
JASPER	REED

SAWYER

SEBASTIAN

SIMON

SPENCER

THEO

TOBIAS

TRUMAN

WALKER

WYATT

COOLEST
VICTORIAN
NAME

· · ·

Thaddeus

true

Bye-bye to the bland connectives of generations past—the ubiquitous Ann that almost sounded like "and"—because the middle name has now taken on a much more active part in the naming process. For one thing, many moms are choosing to use their maiden names in that slot, instead of the bulkier hyphenated names popular in the early days of feminism. It also can be a good place for being creative or whimsical by, say, using a traditional boy's name as a girl's middle (e.g., Max, Ira, George) or something even farther out, such as Aphrodite or Zenobia. Mostly, though, parents are seeking more vivid single-syllable options—many of them drawn from nature—to replace the old Lynns, Lees, Jos, Sues, and Anns. Here are a few ideas primarily for girls:

BAY	BREE
BECK	BRIGHT
BELLE	BRYN
BLUE	CHAN

CLAUDE	MAEVE
DAY	MAIZE
DOE	MAME
DOT	MARCH
DOVE	MAUVE
DREAM	MAX
DUNE	MUSE
FAY	NEAL
FLEUR	NEVE
FLYNN	PAZ
FROST	PEARL
GRAY	PINE
GROVE	PLUM
JADE	POE
JAMES	RAIN
JAZ	REESE
JUDE	SAGE
KAI	SCOUT
KIT	SNOW
LAKE	TEAL
LARK	TRUE
LIL	WREN
LIV	

COOL NICKNAMES

Suddenly, nickname names are cool again. Not the cutesy Cindys and Mindys, Candys and Randis of the '60s and '70s, but rather older, funkier diminutives with a Victorian pedigree. It's a trend that gathered steam in Britain. Some of their favorites are just beginning to land on our shores, but others have already hit our popularity list. Among those that you can consider putting directly on the birth certificate are:

girls

ABBY	DIXIE	FLORRIE
ADDIE	DOT	FRANKIE
AGGIE	DREA	FRANNY
BEA	DREE	FRITZIE
BILLIE	DRU	GIGI
BREE	EDIE	GRACIE
CASSIE	ELLIE	IZZY
CLEO	EMME/EMMY	JAZ/JAZZ
COCO	EVIE	JOHNNIE
DAISY	FIFI	JOSIE

JULES	SUKEY	JEB
KAT	TAY	JED
KATE	TESSIE	JOHNNY
KATIE	TILLIE/TILLY	JUD
KIKI	VINNIE	KIT
KITTY	VIVI	LEM
LETTIE/LETTY		LEV
LIBBY	boys	LEX
LIL	ALFIE	LOUIE
LIV	ARCHIE	MAC
LIVIA	ART	MICK
LOTTIE	ASH	MISHA
LOU	BARNEY	MOE
LULU	BECK	NAT
MAISIE	BENNO	NATE
MAMIE	BERTIE	NED
MILLIE	BILLY	NICO
MINNIE	CAL	OZZIE
MITZI	CHARLIE	PADDY
MO	CHAZ	RAFE
NELLIE	CLEM	RAY
NESSA	DEX	SULLY
PIPPA	DEZI	THEO
POLLY	FREDDIE	TRU
PRU	GEORGIE	TY
ROSIE	GUS	VAN
SADIE	HAL	WILL
SAM	HANK	XAN/ZAN/ZANDER
SASHA	JAX	

Then there's another group of nicknames, those that were used in distant past eras and are all but forgotten now. The following might be worth a fresh look:

girls

BETTA	Elizabeth
BIDU	Bridget
CAM	Camilla
CARO	Caroline
CAT	Catherine
CHARTY	Charlotte
CIA	Cynthia
CINDA	Lucinda, Cynthia
DEBS/DEBO	Deborah
DOE	Dorothea
DORO	Dorothy, Dorothea
FEE	Fiona
FLORY	Florence
FRANCE	Frances

FRITZI	Frederica
IBBY	Isabel
IMMY	Imogen
LEX	Alexis
LOLO	Caroline
MABS	Mabel
MAGO	Margaret
MELIA	Amelia
OUISA	Louise/Louisa
PATIA	Patricia
RIA	Maria
TANSY	Anastasia
TIBBIE	Elizabeth

boys

BAZ	Basil
BRAM	Abraham
CHAN	Chandler
COZ	Cosmo
DASH	Dashiell
DEZ/DEZI	Desmond
DIX	Richard
DUNN	Duncan
GORE	Gordon
GRAM	Graham
JEM	Jeremy
LAURO	Laurence
LENO	Leonard

MANO	Emanuel
MASO	Thomas
PIP	Philip
SEB	Sebastian
SIM/SIMMS	Simeon, Simon
TAD/TADDEO	Theodore
WILLS	William

cool cool

FAMOUS NAMES

kanye

CELEBRITY NAMES

A cool name seems as essential an ingredient of stardom today as a well-sculpted body and a killer smile, a fact that can hardly be lost on parents in search of a name that will help launch their child in the world. Some celebrity names—Keira, Scarlett, and Sienna are notable examples—are inspiring thousands of namesakes, but their real power as a group is in making parents feel that, when it comes to names, special means beautiful, talented, and famous. While names of current stars are most influential, some favorites from the past—Audrey, for instance—are also proving inspirational.

ADRIAN Grenier

AISHA Taylor

AMERICA Ferrera

AMERIE

ANANDA Lewis

ANASTACIA

ANDERSON Cooper

ANGELINA Jolie

ARDEN Wohl

ASHANTI

ASHTON Kutcher

AUDREY Hepburn

AVA Gardner

AVRIL Lavigne

BAI Ling

BALTHAZAR Getty

BECK	DIDO
BENICIO Del Toro	DIVA Zappa
BEYONCÉ Knowles	DJIMON Hounsou
BJÖRK	DOUGRAY Scott
BLU Cantrell	DREA De Matteo
BONO	DREW Barrymore
BRECKIN Meyer	DULÉ Hill
BRYCE Dallas Howard	ELISHA Cuthbert
BYRDIE Bell	ELLE Macpherson
CALISTA Flockhart	EMO Philips
CAMERON Diaz	ENRIQUE Iglesias
CATE Blanchett	ENYA
CHAN Marshall	ESAI Morales
CHARISMA Carpenter	EVA Green/Longoria/Mendes
CHARLIZE Theron	EVANGELINE Lilly
CHINA Chow	EWAN McGregor
CHLOË Sevigny	FAIRUZA Balk
CIARA	FAMKE Janssen
CILLIAN Murphy	FANTASIA
CLEA DuVall	FERGIE
CONAN O'Brien	GARCELLE Beauvais-Nilon
CRISPIN Glover	GISELE Bündchen
CUBA Gooding Jr.	GWYNETH Paltrow
DANE Cook	HALLE Berry
DAX Shepard	Jean HARLOW
DEMI Moore	HAYDEN (male) Christensen
DENZEL Washington	HAYDEN (female) Panettiere
DERMOT Mulroney	HEATH Ledger

IBEN Hjejle

IOAN Gruffudd

IONE Skye

ISLA Fisher

IVANKA Trump

JACINDA Barrett

JADA Pinkett Smith

JAMES King (female)

JAVIER Bardem

JENA Malone

JOAQUIN Phoenix

Angelina JOLIE

JOSS Stone

JUDE Law

KANYE West

KEANU Reeves

KEIRA Knightley

KIEFER Sutherland

KYLIE Minogue

LAKE Bell

LEELEE Sobieski

LEONARDO DiCaprio

LIAM Neeson

LIEV Schreiber

LIV Tyler

Jennifer LOVE Hewitt

MACY Gray

MARIAH Carey

MARISKA Hargitay

MELANIA Trump

MENA Suvari

MILEY Cyrus (born Destiny)

MILLA Jovovich

MINNIE Driver

MISCHA Barton

MOBY

MONET Mazur

NEVE Campbell

NIA Long

NICOLLETTE Sheridan

NIGELLA Lawson

OLIVIER Martinez

OMAR Epps

ORLANDO Bloom

PARIS Hilton

PARKER Posey

PAZ Vega

PENÉLOPE Cruz

PENN Jillette

PETRA Nemcova

PINK

PLUM Sykes

POPPY Montgomery

PORTIA de Rossi

RAINN Wilson

REESE Witherspoon

RIHANNA	TÉA Leoni
ROMANY Malco	THANDIE Newton
ROSARIO Dawson	THORA Birch
SADE	TIGER Woods
SADIE Frost	TILDA Swinton
SAFFRON Burrows	TINSLEY Mortimer
SALMA Hayek	TRACE Adkins
SANAA Latham	TRAYLOR Howard
SANJAYA Malakar	TRENT Reznor
SAVION Glover	TRISTA Sutter
SCARLETT Johansson	TYRA Banks
SHAKIRA	UMA Thurman
SHALOM Harlow	VENUS Williams
SHIA LaBeouf	VIGGO Mortensen
SIENNA Miller	VIN Diesel
SOLEDAD O'Brien	VING Rhames
STELLAN Skarsgård	VIVICA Fox
SUMMER Phoenix	ZAKK Wylde
TALISA Soto	ZIYI Zhang
TAYE Diggs	ZOOEY Deschanel

COOLEST
GLAMOUR GIRL
NAME

• • •

Harlow

vesper

MOVIE-CHARACTER NAMES

The only names cooler than stars' names right now are the names of the characters they play. In fact, with the exception of Jack, which has long seemed to be the name of the male character in every other movie and TV adventure show, characters' names veer from the unusual to the outlandish. A few, such as Trinity from *The Matrix,* jumped right onto the popularity charts. Others may prove inspirational to you. Here is sampling of cool character names, along with the stars who play them and the films in which they appear.

AKASHA	Aaliyah	*Queen of the Damned*
AMÉLIE	Audrey Tautou	*Amélie*
AMIDALA	Natalie Portman	*Star Wars II—Attack of the Clones*
AMSTERDAM	Leonardo DiCaprio	*Gangs of New York*
ARWEN	Liv Tyler	*The Lord of the Rings*
AZRAEL	Jason Lee	*Dogma*
BARTLEBY	Ben Affleck	*Dogma*
	Crispin Glover	*Bartleby*

BELLATRIX	Helena Bonham Carter	*Harry Potter and the Order of the Phoenix*
BJERGEN	Drew Barrymore	*Wayne's World 2*
BONANZA	Rain Phoenix	*Even Cowgirls Get the Blues*
BULLSEYE	Colin Farrell	*Daredevil*
CASH	Don Cheadle	*The Family Man*
CASTOR	John Travolta/ Nicolas Cage	*Face/Off*
CHAKA	Chris Rock	*Jay and Silent Bob Strike Back*
CHASE	Nicole Kidman	*Batman Forever*
CHESNEY	Joey Lauren Adams	*Harvard Man*
CHILI	John Travolta	*Get Shorty*
CHRISTABEL	Jennifer Ehle	*Possession*
CISCO	Mark Addy	*Down to Earth*
CLERICK	Christian Bale	*Equilibrium*
CLOVE	Jennifer Aniston	*The Thin Pink Line*
CLOVER	Angelina Jolie	*The Good Shepherd*
CODY	Elisabeth Shue	*Bad Girls*
COTTON	Liev Schreiber	*Scream 2*
CYRUS	Selma Blair	*Down to You*
DEMILLE	Robert Sean Leonard	*Driven*
DESI	Julia Stiles	*O*
DEVLIN	George Clooney	*Spy Kids*
DOMINO	Keira Knightley	*Domino*

DOVA	Matt Dillon	*Albino Alligator*
DRAVEN	Cuba Gooding Jr.	*In the Shadows*
ELEKTRA	Jennifer Garner	*Daredevil*
ELLE	Reese Witherspoon	*Legally Blonde*
ELMO	Samuel L. Jackson	*Formula 51*
EMIRA	Lela Rochon	*Why Do Fools Fall in Love*
ETHNE	Kate Hudson	*The Four Feathers*
EVANNA	Jessica Capshaw	*Minority Report*
FAIRCHILD	Amy Poehler	*Blades of Glory*
FLINT	Thomas Haden Church	*Spider-Man 3*
FLOR	Paz Vega	*Spanglish*
GRAY	Jennifer Garner	*Catch & Release*
GREEN	Shalom Harlow	*How to Lose a Guy in 10 Days*
HANSEL	Owen Wilson	*Zoolander*
HUCK	Eric Bana	*Lucky You*
IMOGEN	Julia Stiles	*Down to You*
JERZY	George Clooney	*Welcome to Collinwood*
JINX	Halle Berry	*Die Another Day*
JJAKS	Keanu Reeves	*Feeling Minnesota*
JUBA	Djimon Hounsou	*Gladiator*
KAENA	Kirsten Dunst	*Kaena: The Prophecy*
KALE	Shia LaBeouf	*Disturbia*
KORBEN	Bruce Willis	*The Fifth Element*
LAMIA	Michelle Pfeiffer	*Stardust*
LEGOLAS	Orlando Bloom	*The Lord of the Rings*

LIDDA	Kirsten Dunst	*Luckytown Blues*
LOKI	Matt Damon	*Dogma*
LONGFELLOW	Adam Sandler	*Mr. Deeds*
LOTTO	Eric Bana	*The Nugget*
LUSSURIOSO	Eddie Izzard	*Revengers Tragedy*
LUX	Kirsten Dunst	*The Virgin Suicides*
MAXIMUS	Russell Crowe	*Gladiator*
MIDNITE	Djimon Hounsou	*Constantine*
MIRTHA	Penélope Cruz	*Blow*
MORPHEUS	Laurence Fishburne	*The Matrix*
NACHO	Jack Black	*Nacho Libre*
NAPOLEON	Jon Heder	*Napoleon Dynamite*
NEO	Keanu Reeves	*The Matrix*
NIOBE	Jada Pinkett Smith	*Enter the Matrix*
NOLA	Scarlett Johansson	*Match Point*
OBERON	Heath Ledger	*Paws*
OLIVE	Abigail Breslin	*Little Miss Sunshine*
ORORO	Halle Berry	*X-Men*
PADMÉ AMIDALA	Natalie Portman	*Star Wars II—Attack of the Clones*
PELAGIA	Penélope Cruz	*Captain Corelli's Mandolin*
PETAL	Cate Blanchett	*The Shipping News*
PETUNIA	Fiona Shaw	*Harry Potter* series
PISTACHIO	Dana Carvey	*The Master of Disguise*
PLUTO	Eddie Murphy	*The Adventures of Pluto Nash*
POLEXIA	Anna Paquin	*Almost Famous*

RHEYA	Natascha McElhone	*Solaris*
ROUX	Johnny Depp	*Chocolat*
SALA	Catherine Zeta-Jones	*The Phantom*
SATINE	Nicole Kidman	*Moulin Rouge*
SECUS	Rupert Everett	*Stardust*
SERENDIPITY	Salma Hayek	*Dogma*
SERLEENA	Lara Flynn Boyle	*Men in Black II*
SHEBA	Cate Blanchett	*Notes on a Scandal*
SHMALLY	Rachael Leigh Cook	*Scorched*
STEENA	Debi Mazar	*The Tuxedo*
SULLIVAN	Richard Gere	*Dr. T & the Women*
TERRA	Rain Phoenix	*Façade*
TORRANCE	Kirsten Dunst	*Bring It On*
TRINITY	Carrie-Anne Moss	*The Matrix*
TRIP	Josh Hartnett	*The Virgin Suicides*
ULYSSES	George Clooney	*O Brother, Where Art Thou?*
VENOM	Topher Grace	*Spider-Man 3*
VESPER	Eva Green	*Casino Royale*
VIVI	Ashley Judd	*Divine Secrets of the Ya-Ya Sisterhood*
WOLVERINE	Hugh Jackman	*X-Men*
WOO	Jada Pinkett Smith	*Woo*
WREN	Elijah Wood	*Black and White*
XXXX	Daniel Craig	*Layer Cake*
YVAINE	Claire Danes	*Stardust*

| ZEE | Maggie Gyllenhaal | *Monster House* |
| ZINAIDA | Kirsten Dunst | *All Forgotten* |

**COOLEST
COWBOY NAME**

· · ·

Destry

bree

TV-CHARACTER NAMES

ADDISON	*Grey's Anatomy, Private Practice*
ADRIANA	*The Sopranos*
ALEXX	*CSI: Miami*
AMALIA	*Cane*
ARI	*Entourage*
ATIA	*Rome*
BREE	*Desperate Housewives*
CALLIE	*Grey's Anatomy*
CONRAD	*Weeds*
DEXTER	*Dexter*
DRAMA (nickname)	*Entourage*
EDIE	*Desperate Housewives*
ELLIOT (female)	*Scrubs*
GABRIELLE	*Desperate Housewives*
HIRO	*Heroes*
HORATIO	*CSI: Miami*
ISAAC	*Heroes*
ISOBEL/IZZIE	*Grey's Anatomy*

JACK	*24, Lost*
LENNOX	*24*
LIBERTY	*Degrassi: The Next Generation*
LOCKE	*Lost*
LUCIUS	*Rome*
MEREDITH	*Grey's Anatomy*
MICAH	*Heroes*
MIRANDA	*Grey's Anatomy*
NICOLETTE	*Big Love*
OCTAVIA	*Rome*
ODAFIN (FIN)	*Law & Order: Special Victims Unit*
PRESTON	*Grey's Anatomy*
ROMAN	*Big Love*
SAWYER	*Lost*
SHARPAY	*High School Musical 2*
SILAS	*Weeds*
TANCY	*Big Love*
TEYLA	*Stargate Atlantis*
TITUS	*Rome*
TRIPP	*Dirty Sexy Money*
TURTLE (nickname)	*Entourage*
WILHELMINA	*Ugly Betty*

kazooie

VIDEO GAME NAMES

Movie- and TV-character names may seem both inspired and inspirational to parents at the beginning of the twenty-first century, but what of the next generation of parents-to-be, those raised not on movies and television but on video games? Their idea of a cool name is sure to be way wilder than that of parents today. These names from popular video games will give you an idea of the kind of choices that could inspire the names of your grandchildren.

girls

AERITH	PAI
AOI	PAINE
ASTAROTH	QUISTIS
BLOODRAYNE	RIKKU
CORTANA	RINOA
JAHEIRA	RYNN
KAIRI	SAMUS
LARA	SELPHIE

SHION	KAGE
SHODAN	KAIN
SORA	KAZOOIE
TAKI	KIALOS
TIFA	KLONOA
YUNA	LINK
	MAJORA
boys	MAXIMO
AIDYN	MUNCH
AKUJI	PARAPPA
ALUCARD	RAIDEN
ARC	RYGAR
BANJO	RYU
CLOUD	SPYRO
CRASH	SQUALL
DAXTER	TIDUS
DING	TOAN
GOEMON	VYSE
GOKU	YOSHI
ICO	ZELL
JAK	ZIDAN
JOJO	

tennyson

CELEBRITY BABY NAMES

Baby naming has come to be a competitive sport in Hollywood. The goal: to come up with the coolest name in town—a difficult task when your colleagues' babies are named Shiloh (Angelina Jolie & Brad Pitt), Suri (Katie Holmes & Tom Cruise), and Apple (Gwyneth Paltrow & Chris Martin).

So what are we poor mortals to do, hearing such curious names? If not follow suit by naming our own children Shiloh and Suri, then at least feel inspired to be a bit more adventurous in our own choices of names. Just as celebrities influence our taste in clothes and hair and makeup, so too do they give us a new model for baby naming.

Here are the coolest celebrity baby names of recent years, the famous parents who chose them, along with our thinking on why the names belong in this category.

ALICE ZENOBIA • Tina Fey
A creative pairing that works: the sweet classic Alice coupled with an exotic rarity.

APPLE • Gwyneth Paltrow & Chris Martin

This celebrity couple set off international shock waves when they chose this wholesome, rosy-cheeked fruit name for their daughter, but we can see it starting a trend—with Plums, Peaches, Berrys, Cherrys, and even Lemons, Mangos, and Papayas possibly populating future schoolrooms.

ATLANTA NOO • Amanda de Cadenet & John Taylor

What's noo? Atlanta is one of the fresher-sounding place names, as are Avalon and Alabama.

ATTICUS • Isabella Hoffman & Daniel Baldwin

A name so weighty it becomes almost whimsical, associated by most people with the noble lawyer played by Gregory Peck in the classic *To Kill a Mockingbird*.

AUDREY • Faith Hill & Tim McGraw/Greg Kinnear

A name that reflects the luminous star power of the radiant Audrey Hepburn, now making a strong comeback.

AUGUST • Mariska Hargitay/Jeanne Tripplehorn

A German and Scandinavian classic becomes a newly favored month of the year—mostly for boys but occasionally for girls as well.

AURELIUS • Elle Macpherson

Given the supermodel seal of approval, this is one of the band of Roman emperor names now in the realm of possibility.

AVA • Aidan Quinn/Heather Locklear & Richie Sambora/John McEnroe/Reese Witherspoon & Ryan Phillippe/Hugh Jackman/Martina McBride/Mia Hamm/Kevin Dillon/Jason Priestley

Radiating the sultry retro glamour of Ava Gardner, and propelled by its hot celebrity-favorite status, this name has made a spectacular climb up the popularity charts for parents across the board.

AVERY • Angie Harmon & Jason Sehorn

A true unisex name, growing in popularity for both the pinks and the blues.

BARRON • Melania & Donald Trump

The Donald ordained his latest offspring a nobleperson from the get-go.

BECKETT • Malcolm McDowell/Natalie Maines/Melissa Etheridge/Conan O'Brien

An appealing surname name rich in literary associations, both to the play and movie based on the life of Thomas à Becket and to the Irish playwright-novelist Samuel Beckett, it's red-hot in Hollywood.

BLUEBELL MADONNA • Geri Halliwell

Bluebell, though undeniably sweet and original, may be trying so hard for coolness that it just doesn't achieve it. Ditto Madonna.

CLARA • Ewan McGregor

Just as Americans are rediscovering Claire, leave it to a Brit to home in on its quainter-sounding variation. His other daughter is called the equally neglected Esther.

COCO • Courtney Cox & David Arquette

Though it has some fashion power via legendary designer Chanel, Coco, like high-kicking friends Kiki, Gigi, and Fifi, has lots of Gallic spirit but is short on substance.

CRUZ • Victoria Adams & David Beckham

For a third time, following Brooklyn and Romeo, the Beckhams caused quite a stir when they chose this unisex Latino surname for their youngest son. It packs a good deal of energy, charm, and sex appeal into its single syllable.

DASHIELL • Cate Blanchett

A lot of dash and a touch of mystery thanks to classic detective writer Dashiell Hammett.

DIXIE • Tabitha Soren

Wisecracking waitress, saucy Southern showgirl.

DREAM • Sole & Ginuwine

This contemporary music duo chose two dreamy but cutting-edge word names for their daughters: Dream and Story.

EDEN • Marcia Cross

Savannah's twin sister was given the primal place name.

ESME • Tracy Pollan & Michael J. Fox/Samantha Morton/
Anthony Edwards/Katey Sagal

A captivating J. D. Salinger–inspired choice.

FINLEY • Chris O'Donnell/Holly Marie Combs

One of the newly popular Fin-family names, which also includes
Finn (Christy Turlington & Ed Burns/Jane Leeves) and Finnegan
(Eric McCormack), not to mention Phinnaeus (Julia Roberts).

FRANCES PEN • Amanda Peet

An old-fashioned name made more daring because it's only recently come out of mothballs, and made more modern with the
addition of the catchy short form of grandma's name, Penny.

GABLE NESS • Kevin Nealon

If the girls can have Harlow, why not Gable for the boys?

GOD'ISS LOVE • Lil' Mo

Some parents—especially those of the rapper persuasion—are
moving beyond such religious/spiritual names as Genesis, Trinity, Miracle, Heaven, and Nevaeh (heaven spelled backward) to
more extreme examples like this and Praise Mary (DNX).

HAZEL • Julia Roberts

A gentle green-eyed oldie with newly bestowed star power.

IRIS • Sadie Frost & Jude Law

Floral names like Rose and Lily are spreading like wildflowers,
but the high-profile parents of Rafferty and Rudy dared to pick

a bloom that had been long out of fashion and make it sound fresh again.

KAL-EL • Nicolas Cage

Superman's Kryptonian birth name is unlikely to impart superhuman qualities to any mortal boy.

KINGSTON • Gwen Stefani & Gavin Rossdale

This Jamaican place name (where the No Doubt couple was recording a couple of years ago) and elegant British surname also boasts the more regal yet user-friendly short form, King.

LOLA • Annie Lennox/Kelly Ripa/Chris Rock/Denise Richards & Charlie Sheen/Carnie Wilson/Kim Dean

Madonna's use of Lola as the nickname for her daughter, Lourdes, brought this name from the smoky back room to center stage in terms of style. (Other lilting double-*l* names: Lila (Kate Moss) and Lily (Kate Beckinsale, Chris O'Donnell, Johnny Depp).

MAGNUS • Will Ferrell/Kirsty Swanson

The Latin root of this name brings it into the newly trendy Little Caesar category of upright and imposing appellations dating back to the Roman Empire.

MALACHY • Cillian Murphy

An Irish version of a biblical name, with an expansive, almost boisterous image.

MATILDA • Michelle Williams & Heath Ledger/Moon Unit Zappa

So far out it's in possibility with Aussie connections, might be slated for a comeback after being picked by this once high-profile couple and then by one of the original oddly named starbabies.

MERCY • Andy Richter

A lovely, neglected colonial virtue name. As her daddy said, "Just in case Puritanism comes back, we'll be ready with a real pilgrim name."

MILLER • Stella McCartney/Melissa Etheridge

An appealing up-and-coming new occupational surname choice.

MILO • Ricki Lake/Camryn Manheim/Liz Tyler/Sherry Stringfield

Jaunty.

MOSES • Gwyneth Paltrow & Chris Martin

Venerable, white-bearded Old Testament name brought into the twenty-first century as Apple's brother.

MOXIE CRIMEFIGHTER • Penn Jillette

The first name has plenty of, well, moxie. Dad's excuse for the second: "When she's pulled over for speeding, she can say, 'But officer, we're on the same side, my middle name is CrimeFighter.'" Though she'll probably have dropped it by then.

ORSON • Paz Vega/Lauren Ambrose

Following in the wake of Oscar, Orson is a newly fashionable *O* name.

PAX THIEN • Angelina Jolie & Brad Pitt

The embodiment of peace.

PIPER • Gillian Anderson/Brian De Palma/Cuba Gooding Jr./ Samantha Bee

High energy and musicality.

POPPY HONEY • *Naked Chef* Jamie Oliver

Poppy is cool, Honey a little gooey, when combined they sound more like recipe ingredients than a name.

RAFFERTY • Sadie Frost & Jude Law

One of the coolest of the Irish surnames, with a raffish quality all its own.

RAMONA • Maggie Gyllenhaal & Peter Sarsgaard

A fresh choice that combines the charm of the children's book heroine with an exotically sultry quality.

ROAN • Sharon Stone

A strong, red-haired Irish name.

ROMAN • Cate Blanchett/Debra Messing/Harvey Keitel

A surprise hit in recent years, both muscular and slightly exotic.

ROMEO • Victoria Adams & David Beckham/Jon Bon Jovi

Romeo, Romeo, wherefore art thou? Thou art a previously quasi-taboo, overly dramatic Shakespearean exclusive that's now been legitimized as a baby-name possibility.

ROMY • Matt Lauer/Sofia Coppola

A German shortening of Rosemary, exotic but energetic.

RUBY • Matthew Modine/Suzanne Vega/Rod Stewart/Tobey Maguire

This vibrant red jewel of a name is sassy and sultry, and definitely on the rise.

SADIE • Joan Allen/Adam Sandler

Onetime grandma name becomes cool and feisty baby name.

SAM ALEXIS • Tiger Woods

More and more girls are being given the nickname of Samantha on their birth certificates; this one pays tribute to the golfing great's dad, whose nickname for his son was Sam.

SHILOH NOUVEL • Angelina Jolie & Brad Pitt

First name is a biblical/Civil War place name meaning "God's gift"; the second is the surname of one of Dad Brad's favorite architects.

STORY ELIAS • Jenna Elfman

One of the best of the evocative new word names makes a newsworthy substitute for Cory or Rory.

SULLIVAN • Patrick Dempsey

A jaunty Irish surname name with a real twinkle in its eye.

SURI • Katie Holmes & Tom Cruise

This obscure multicultural name hit the headlines as the daughter of TomKat, provoking heated debate among name experts as to its actual meaning. Is it "princess" or "go away" in Hebrew? "Pointy nose" in an Indian dialect? "Pickpocket" in Japanese? All of the above?

TENNYSON • Russell Crowe

Intriguing, original, poetic choice.

THIJS • Matt Lauer

What is thijs? It's a Dutch boy's name pronounced *tice*— common in the Netherlands but a rarity here.

TRUE • Forest Whitaker/Joely Fisher

Inspirational, aspirational word name that works particularly well as a middle name. Fisher named her daughter True Harlow: a real trend blend.

VIOLET • Jennifer Garner & Ben Affleck/Dave Grohl

Soft and sweet but not shrinking, Victorian Violet, one of the prettiest of color and flower names, has begun what is certain to be a rapid rise to popularity.

ZOLTEN • Penn Jillette

Moxie CrimeFighter's younger brother was given his mother's maiden name—which also happens to be the name of Dracula's dog.

COOLEST
FRUIT NAME

• • •

Plum

augustin

SUPERMODEL BABY NAMES

It's not enough that they're skinny, gorgeous, world-revered millionaires. They've got babies, too—and not just ordinary babies, but babies with incredibly cool names. Here is the recent crop of supermodel baby names:

AMAEL (boy)	Audrey Marnay
ARPAD FLYNN	Elle Macpherson
ARTHUR ELOD	Jasmine Guinness
AUDEN (boy)	Amber Valletta
AUGUSTIN JAMES	Linda Evangelista
AURELIUS CY	Elle Macpherson
CASPAR	Claudia Schiffer
CECILY	Stella Tennant
CLEMENTINE	Claudia Schiffer
DYLAN BLUE (girl)	Carolyn Murphy
ELLA	Lucie de la Falaise
ELLA RAE	Rhea Durham
FINN	Christy Turlington
FRANKIE-JEAN	Donna D'Errico

GRACE	Christy Turlington
HAMZAH (boy)	Yasmine Warsame
HENRY	Heidi Klum
IRIS	Stella Tennant
JASMINE	Stella Tennant
JOHAN RILEY FYODOR TAIWO	Heidi Klum
KAIA JORDAN	Cindy Crawford
LENI	Heidi Klum
LILA GRACE	Kate Moss
LUCAS	Cecilia Chancellor/Natalia Vodianova
MARCEL	Stella Tennant
MINGUS LUCIEN	Helena Christensen
NEVA	Natalia Vodianova
NIMA (boy)	Trish Goff
ORSON	Lucie de la Falaise
PRESLEY	Cindy Crawford
RAEE (girl)	Liya Kebede
SAFFRON SAHARA	Yasmin Le Bon
SAHTEENE	Laetitia Costa
SCYLER PIM (girl)	Frederique van der Wal
SKYLA LILY LAKE	Liberty Ross
SUHUL (boy)	Liya Kebede
TALLULAH PINE	Yasmin Le Bon
TOBY COLE	Emme
WILLIAM DAKOTA	Angela Lindvall
YANNICK FAUSTO	Daniela Pestova

agyness

SUPERMODEL NAMES

And what about the supermodel moms themselves? Their names are at least as exotic as those they give their kids, providing a real international smorgasbord of choices.

ADINA	EGLE
AGYNESS	EKAT
ALANA	ESTELLA
ALYONA	FLAVIA
ANJA	FREDERIQUE
BEHATI	FREJA
BETTE	GEMMA
BRUNA	HANA
CAPRICE	HONORINE
CHANEL	HYE
CICELY	IEKELIENE
COCO	IRINA
DARYA	ISELIN
DOUTZEN	JEISA

KASIA

KINGA

LAETITIA

LARA

LARAGH

LILY

LIYA

MAGDALENA

MALGOSIA

MARINA

MILANA

NATALIA

NATASHA

OLGA

OLYA

RAQUEL

ROMINA

SASHA

SERAFIMA

SHALOM

SNEJANA

SOFI

SOLANGE

SUVI

TATJANA

TILU

VLADA

YFKE

christo

Artists (and architects and designers) are almost by definition cool, and their names are often part of the package. Parents can capture some of that creative spirit by choosing one of these artist names for their baby—and at the same time give their child an inspirational role model. The following list encompasses both first (JASPER Johns) and last (Alexander CALDER) names, which have been drawn from all over the aesthetic map.

AALTO	BOHAN	CLAES
ALAIA	BRAQUE	COCO
AMEDEO	CALDER	COLE
ANGELICO	CARO	CONRAN
ANSEL	CELLINI	CORNELL
ANSELM	CHANEL	COROT
ARMANI	CHARDIN	CRISTOBAL
AZZEDINE	CHIRICO	CURRAN
BLAKE	CHRISTO	CURRIER

CY	IVES	MIRÓ
DELAUNAY	JACKSON	MIUCCIA
DIX	JASPER	MONET
DONATELLA	JENSEN	MOORE
DONATELLO	JUDD	MORANDI
DUCCIO	KAHLO	MOREAU
DUFY	KAMALI	MORI
EAMES	KENZO	MORISOT
EERO	KIEFER	NEO
ELLIS	KIKI	NOUVEL
FORD	KLEE	O'KEEFFE
FRIDA	KRIZIA	PABLO
GABO	LAUTREC	PALOMA
GAUGUIN	LEGER	PEI
GEHRY	LEONARDO	PELLI
GEORGIA	LOEWY	PENN
GERRIT	MAGRITTE	PIANO
GOYA	MAILLOL	PICABIA
GRECO	MANET	PICASSO
HARDY	MANOLO	PIET
HARTIGAN	MANZU	PONTI
HERMES	MARDEN	QUANT
HOMER	MARIN	RABANNE
HOPPER	MARISOL	RAEBURN
IMOGEN	MATTA	RAPHAEL
INDIANA	MIES	REM
INIGO	MILLAIS	REMINGTON
ISSEY	MILLET	ROBBIA

RODIN	TAMAYO	VINCENT
ROUSSEAU	TITIAN	VIONNET
RYDER	TOULOUSE	WESTON
SARGENT	TURNER	WILLEM
SERRA	VALENTINA	WINSLOW
SHAHN	VALENTINO	YVES
SIMONETTA	VENTURI	ZANDRA
SOUTINE	VIEIRA	
SULLY	VIGEE	

hendrix

MUSICIAN NAMES

Since musicians invented the concept of cool, where better to look for naming inspiration than to their own names?

AALIYAH	AXL	BONO
ABBA	BAEZ	BOWIE
ADEMA	BASIE	BRAHMS
AJA	BECHET	CAB
ALANIS	BECK	CALE
ALANNAH	BENATAR	CALLAS
AMADEUS	BESSIE	CALLOWAY
ARETHA	BEYONCÉ	CARUSO
ARLO	BILLIE	CHAKA
ARMSTRONG	BING	COLE
ASHANTI	BIX	COLTRANE
AUDRA	BJÖRK	COOLIO
AVRIL	BLU	CROSBY

DENVER GILLESPIE MILES
DEVO GUTHRIE MINGUS
DEXTER HARRISON MORRISON
DINAH HENDRIX MORRISSEY
DION IGGY MOZART
DIXIE JABBO MULLIGAN
DJANGO (the *D* is JACKSON MYA
silent) JAGGER NASH
DONOVAN JAHEIM NAT
DUFF JOPLIN NELLY
DURAN JOSS NICA
DYLAN KAI NIRVANA
EARTHA KANYE ODETTA
ELLINGTON KELIS OTIS
ELTON KITT OZZY
ELVIS LATIFAH PEARL
ENO LENNON PIAF
ENRIQUE LENNOX PINK
ENYA LIONEL PLACIDO
ETTA LOUDON PRESLEY
EVERLY LOUIS PRINCE
FABIAN LUCIANO QUINCY
FABRIZIO MACY RAMONE
FERGIE MADONNA RAVI
GARCIA MAHALIA RAY
GARTH MARIAH RIHANNA
GENESIS MARLEY RUFUS
GERSHWIN MEHTA SADE

SANTANA	TALIB	WOLFGANG
SHAKIRA	THELONIOUS	WYCLEF
SHANIA	USHER	WYNTON
SINÉAD	VEGA	ZEVON
SULLIVAN	VERDI	ZUBIN

COOLEST
COUNTRY MUSIC
NAME

• • •

Paisley

chamillionaire

RAP NAMES

Names of rappers take the galaxy of possibilities into a whole other universe, one that few parents, at least right now, will want to visit. Not to be too academic about this, but rap names have their basis in the double-naming tradition that dates back to the very beginnings of African-American culture, when slaves used the names imposed by their masters when white folk were around, and other names—African names, day names, nicknames—when they were with friends and family. So while it might be ludicrous at this point to think of naming your child after rapper Ludacris, the boundary-breaking nature of rap names promises to inspire more adventurous choices—even if just for their kids' nicknames—among music-loving parents in the future. Here are a few of the rap names around today:

BIG BOI	BUSTA RHYMES
BIZZY	CHAMILLIONAIRE
BUBBA SPARXXX	CHINGY

CLIPS

COMMON

DANGER MOUSE

DMX

DR. DRE

EAZY E

FABOLOUS

FLAVOR FLAV

ICE CUBE

ICE-T

JA RULE

JAY-Z

J DILLA

LIL BOW WOW

LIL' KIM

LIL SCRAPPY

LIL' ZANE

LUDACRIS

LUMIDEE

MACE

MOS DEF

NAS

NE-YO

SISQÓ

SNOOP DOGG

T-PAIN

UNK

YUNG JOC

pirate

ROCKER AND RAPPER KIDS' NAMES

If you call yourself Ludacris or Slash or Flea, chances are you're not gonna name your kid Matthew or Martha or Mike. In fact, rock-and-roll and hip-hop musicians are probably the most imaginative—or outrageous, depending on your point of view—category of baby namers there is, honoring their musical heroes (Thelonious, Lennon, Hendrix), using words as names (Million, Dream, Zeppelin), or just letting their fantasies fly. To wit:

ACE	Natalie Appleton/Tom (No Doubt) Dumont
ALABAMA	Travis (Blink 182) Barker
ALFIE	Chris (Muse) Wolstenholme
ALZEA	Chingy
ANAIS	Noel (Oasis) Gallagher
ANGEL	Melanie (Spice Girls) Brown
APPLE	Chris (Coldplay) Martin & Gwyneth Paltrow

ARTEMIS	Alex (Blur) James
ATLANTA	John (Duran Duran) Taylor
	& Amanda de Cadenet
BAMBOO	Big Boi (Outkast)
BERTIE (Albert)	Kate Bush
BLUE ANGEL	Dave (The Edge) Evans
BLUEBELL **MADONNA**	Geri (Spice Girls) Halliwell
CASH	Saul "Slash" (Guns N' Roses) Hudson
CASPAR	James (Metallica) Hetfield
CASSIUS	Richard (The Verve) Ashcroft
COSIMO	Beck
CROSS	Big Boi (Outkast)
CRUZ	Victoria Adams (Spice Girls) &
	David Beckham
CYPRESS (girl)	Sol
DECKER	Nikki Sixx
DJANGO	Siobhan (Bananarama) Fahey &
	Dave Stewart
DOMANI	T.I.
DRAVEN	Chester (Linkin Park) Bennington
DREAM	Sol & Ginuwine
ELMO	Curt (Meat Puppets) Kirkwood
EVERLY BEAR	Anthony (Red Hot Chili Peppers)
	Kiedis
FIRE	Steve Vai
FRANKIE- **JEAN**	Nikki Sixx

FRANKITO	Tré Cool (Green Day)
GERONIMO	Alex (Blur) James
GIACOMO	Sting
GOD'ISS LOVE	Lil' Mo
HAPPY	Macy Gray
HEAVEN	Lil' Mo
HENDRIX	Zakk (Black Label Society) Wylde
HERCY, MERCY, VERCY, & PERCY JR.	Master P
INDIGO	Tom (The Thompson Twins) Bailey
KAMA	Sammy Hagar
KARMA	Ludacris
KING	T.I.
LENNON	Liam (Oasis) Gallagher
LOLITA BOOTSY	Kelly (Stereophonics) Jones
MARQUISE	50 Cent
MEMPHIS	Bono
MESSIAH	T.I.
MILLION	Mystikal (No Limit)
NAVY	Nivea & Terius Nash
NEVAEH	Sonny (P.O.D.) Sandoval
NEVIS	Nelly Furtado
PHOENIX	Melanie (Spice Girls) Brown
PHYNLEY (girl)	Phil (Newsboys) Joel
PIRATE	Fred (Limp Bizkit) Durst
PRAISE MARY	DMX
PUMA	Erykah Badu
REBOP	Todd Rundgren

ROCCO	Madonna
ROMEO	Victoria Adams (Spice Girls) & David Beckham/Jon Bon Jovi
SAFFRON	Simon Le Bon
SAGE	Lars (Metallica) Ulrich
SALVADOR	Ed (Radiohead) O'Brien
SAMARIA	LL Cool J
SEVEN	Erykah Badu & Andre (Andre 3000) Benjamin
SINDRI	Björk
SPECK	John Mellencamp
STORY	Sol & Ginuwine
SUGAR McQUEEN	Nikka Costa
SUNNY BEBOP	Michael "Flea" Balzary (Red Hot Chili Peppers)
TAJ	Steven (Arrowsmith) Tyler
TALLULAH	Simon Le Bon
TENZIN	Adam (Beastie Boys) Yauch
THELONIOUS	Mitch (Crash Test Dummies) Dorge
WOLFGANG	Eddie Van Halen & Valerie Bertinelli
ZEPPELIN	Jonathan (Korn)

auden

LITERARY NAMES

Literary inspiration can arise from both the names of authors and the characters they create. Here are some suggestions coming from the first and last names of writers ranging from Edgar Allan Poe to Zadie Smith, and characters from the pages of books spanning various periods of literary history. In this category, as always, feel free to think about your own personal favorites:

AUTHORS

ALCOTT	AYN
AMIS	BALDWIN
ANAÏS	BALLARD
ANGELOU	BECKETT
APHRA	BEHAN
AUDEN	BELLOW
AUGUST	BENÉT
AUSTEN	BLAKE
AUSTER	BLY

BRONTË	HAMMETT
BYATT	HARPER
BYRON	HART
CAIN	HARTE
CARSON	HEMINGWAY
CARVER	HOMER
CHANDLER	HUGO
CHEEVER	ISHMAEL
CONRAD	JARRELL
COOPER	JERZY
CRANE	JESSAMYN
DANTE	KEATS
DASHIELL	KEROUAC
DIDION	KESEY
DJUNA	LAFCADIO
DYLAN	LALITA
ELIOT	LANGSTON
ELLISON	LARDNER
EMERSON	LE CARRÉ
EUDORA	LIONEL
FITZGERALD	LONDON
FLANNERY	LORCA
FORSTER	LOWELL
FROST	MALLARMÉ
GALWAY	MAYA
GIDE	McEWAN
GLASGOW	MEHTA
GORE	MILAN
HADLEY	MILLAY

MORRISON	SHAW
MOSS	TENNESSEE
MUNRO	TENNYSON
NERUDA	THACKERAY
NIN	THEROUX
NORRIS	THISBE
O'CASEY	THOREAU
PAZ	THURBER
PLATO	TRUMAN
PLUM	TWAIN
POE	VIDAL
RALEIGH	WALKER
RHYS	WILLA
RING	YEATS
ROALD	ZADIE
RUMER	ZANE
SALINGER	ZOLA
SAROYAN	ZORA
SHAKESPEARE	

COOLEST
POET NAME
• • •
Auden

CHARACTERS

female

ALABAMA	*Save Me the Waltz*	Zelda Fitzgerald
ALHAMBRA	*The Accidental*	Ali Smith
ALIA	*Dune*	Frank Herbert
ALMA	*The History of Love*	Nicole Krauss
AMARYLLIS	*Back to Methuselah*	George Bernard Shaw
AMORET	*The Faerie Queene*	Edmund Spenser
ÁNTONIA	*My Ántonia*	Willa Cather
ARABELLA	*Jude the Obscure*	Thomas Hardy
ARIADNE	*Heartbreak House*	George Bernard Shaw
ATALANTA	*Metamorphoses*	Ovid
AURELIUS	*The Thirteenth Tale*	Diane Setterfield
AURORA	*Terms of Endearment*	Larry McMurtry
BATHSHEBA	*Far from the Madding Crowd*	Thomas Hardy
BENNINGTON	*Going Down*	Jennifer Bell
BLUE	*Special Topics in Calamity Physics*	Marisha Pessl
BRETT	*The Sun Also Rises*	Ernest Hemingway
BRIANA	*The Faerie Queene*	Edmund Spenser
BRIONY	*Atonement*	Ian McEwan
CALIXTA	"At the 'Cadian Ball"	Kate Chopin
CALLIOPE	*Middlesex*	Jeffrey Eugenides
	Coyote Blue	Christopher Moore
CATALINA	*The High Road*	Edna O'Brien
CATRIONA	*Catriona*	Robert Louis Stevenson

CHARITY	*Martin Chuzzlewit*	Charles Dickens
CHARMIAN	*Antony and Cleopatra*	William Shakespeare
CLARICE	*The Silence of the Lambs*	Thomas Harris
CLARISSA	*Mrs. Dalloway*	Virginia Woolf
CLEA	*Alexandria Quartet*	Lawrence Durrell
CLELIA	*The Charterhouse of Parma*	Stendhal
COSETTE	*Les Misérables*	Victor Hugo
CRESSIDA	*Troilus and Cressida*	William Shakespeare
DAHLIA	*Carry on, Jeeves*	P. G. Wodehouse
DAISY	*The Great Gatsby*	F. Scott Fitzgerald
DENVER	*Beloved*	Toni Morrison
DESDEMONA	*Othello*	William Shakespeare
	Middlesex	Jeffrey Eugenides
DOMENICA	*Unconditional Surrender*	Evelyn Waugh
ELLIS	*And Now You Can Go*	Vendela Vida
ELVIA	*Highwire Moon*	Susan Straight
EMMA	*Emma*	Jane Austen
ESMÉ	"For Esmé—with Love and Squalor"	J. D. Salinger
EVANGELINE	*Evangeline*	Henry Wadsworth Longfellow
FANCY	*Under the Greenwood Tree*	Thomas Hardy
FAUNIA	*The Human Stain*	Philip Roth
FEATHER	*Bad Boy Brawly Brown*	Walter Mosley
FIG	*The Man of My Dreams*	Curtis Sittenfeld
FLEUR	*The Forsyte Saga*	John Galsworthy

GINEVRA	*Villette*	Charlotte Brontë
GUINEVERE	*King Arthur: Tales of the Round Table*	Andrew Lang (ed.)
HANA	*The English Patient*	Michael Ondaatje
HAYDÉE	*The Count of Monte Cristo*	Alexandre Dumas
HERMIONE	Harry Potter series	J. K. Rowling
HONORA	*Sea Glass*	Anita Shreve
HONORIA	*Bleak House*	Charles Dickens
HYACINTH	*The Princess Casamassima*	Henry James
ISADORA	*Fear of Flying*	Erica Jong
ISOLDE	*Tristan*	Gottfried von Strassburg
JACY	*The Last Picture Show*	Larry McMurtry
JADINE	*Tar Baby*	Toni Morrison
JULIET	*Romeo and Juliet*	William Shakespeare
JUNO	*Juno and the Paycock*	Sean O'Casey
KIKI	*On Beauty*	Zadie Smith
KINSEY	*A is for Alibi,* etc.	Sue Grafton
LAVINIA	*Mourning Becomes Electra*	Eugene O'Neill
LOLITA	*Lolita*	Vladimir Nabokov
LUX	*The Virgin Suicides*	Jeffrey Eugenides
MAISIE	*What Maisie Knew*	Henry James
MALTA	*Bleak House*	Charles Dickens

MAMIE	*The Ambassadors*	Henry James
MARIGOLD	*Quartet in Autumn*	Barbara Pym
MARIN	*A Book of Common Prayer*	Joan Didion
MELANCTHA	*Three Lives*	Gertrude Stein
MERCY	*Martin Chuzzlewit*	Charles Dickens
NARCISSA	*Sartoris*	William Faulkner
NENNA	*Offshore*	Penelope Fitzgerald
NERISSA	*The Merchant of Venice*	William Shakespeare
NINETTA	*Nicholas Nickleby*	Charles Dickens
NIOBE	*Metamorphoses*	Ovid
ORLEANNA	*The Poisonwood Bible*	Barbara Kingsolver
PANSY	*The Portrait of a Lady*	Henry James
PECOLA	*The Bluest Eye*	Toni Morrison
PEYTON	*Lie Down in Darkness*	William Styron
PILAR	*For Whom the Bell Tolls*	Ernest Hemingway
PLEASANT	*Our Mutual Friend*	Charles Dickens
PORTIA	*The Merchant of Venice*	William Shakespeare
PRAIRIE	*Vineland*	Thomas Pynchon
PRECIOUS	*The No. 1 Ladies' Detective Agency*	Alexander McCall Smith
RAIN	*The Sandcastle*	Iris Murdoch

REMARKABLE	*The Pioneers*	James Fenimore Cooper
ROMOLA	*Romola*	George Eliot
ROSAMOND	*Middlemarch*	George Eliot
SAI	*The Inheritance of Loss*	Kiran Desai
SCARLETT	*Gone With the Wind*	Margaret Mitchell
SCOUT	*To Kill a Mockingbird*	Harper Lee
SERAFINA	*Highwire Moon*	Susan Straight
SETHE	*Beloved*	Toni Morrison
SHEBA (BATHSHEBA)	*Notes on a Scandal*	Zoë Heller
SIDDA/ SIDDALEE	*Divine Secrets of the Ya-Ya Sisterhood*	Rebecca Wells
SNOW FLOWER	*Snow Flower and the Secret Fan*	Lisa See
SUGAR	*Pigs in Heaven*	Barbara Kingsolver
SULA	*Sula*	Toni Morrison
SWEENEY	Sweeney St. George mysteries	Sarah Stewart Taylor
TAMORA	*Titus Andronicus*	William Shakespeare
TAMSIN	*A Few Green Leaves*	Barbara Pym
TEMPLE	*Sanctuary*	William Faulkner
UNDINE	*The Custom of the Country*	Edith Wharton
VELVET	*National Velvet*	Enid Bagnold
VERENA	*The Bostonians*	Henry James

VIDA	*The Thirteenth Tale*	Diane Setterfield
	Vida	Marge Piercy
VIVI	*Divine Secrets of the Ya-Ya Sisterhood*	Rebecca Wells
VIVIETTE	*Two on a Tower*	Thomas Hardy
ZENOBIA	*The Blithedale Romance*	Nathaniel Hawthorne
ZORA	*On Beauty*	Zadie Smith
ZULEIKA	*Zuleika Dobson*	Max Beerbohm

male

AMORY	*This Side of Paradise*	F. Scott Fitzgerald
ARAMIS	*The Three Musketeers*	Alexandre Dumas
ARCHER	*The Age of Innocence*	Edith Wharton
ATTICUS	*To Kill a Mockingbird*	Harper Lee
AURIC	*Goldfinger*	Ian Fleming
AXEL	*Victory*	Joseph Conrad
BARLEY	*The Russia House*	John le Carré
BARNABY	*Barnaby Rudge*	Charles Dickens
BEALE	*What Maisie Knew*	Henry James
BENVOLIO	*Romeo and Juliet*	William Shakespeare
BRICK	*Cat on a Hot Tin Roof*	Tennessee Williams
BROM	*The Legend of Sleepy Hollow*	Washington Irving
CALIBAN	*The Tempest*	William Shakespeare
CASPAR	*The Portrait of a Lady*	Henry James
CATO	*Henry and Cato*	Iris Murdoch
CHANCE	*Being There*	Jerzy Koszinski

CLEON	*Pericles*	William Shakespeare
CODY	*Visions of Cody*	Jack Kerouac
CORIN	*As You Like It*	William Shakespeare
CROW	*Kafka on the Shore*	Haruki Murakami
DARCY	*Pride and Prejudice*	Jane Austen
DARL	*As I Lay Dying*	William Faulkner
DORIAN	*The Picture of Dorian Gray*	Oscar Wilde
DUNSTAN	*Silas Marner*	George Eliot
FALMOUTH	*You Don't Love Me Yet*	Jonathan Lethem
FENNO	*Three Junes*	Julia Glass
FITZWILLIAM	*Pride and Prejudice*	Jane Austen
GOGOL	*The Namesake*	Jhumpa Lahiri
GUITAR	*Song of Solomon*	Toni Morrison
GULLIVER	*Gulliver's Travels*	Jonathan Swift
HEATHCLIFF	*Wuthering Heights*	Emily Brontë
HIERONYMOUS/ HARRY	*City of Bones*	Michael Connelly
HOLDEN	*The Catcher in the Rye*	J. D. Salinger
ISHMAEL	*Moby-Dick*	Herman Melville
JAPHY	*Dharma Bums*	Jack Kerouac
JARVIS	*A Tale of Two Cities*	Charles Dickens
JASPER	*The Pathfinder*	James Fenimore Cooper
JOLYON	*The Forsyte Saga*	John Galsworthy
JUDE	*Jude the Obscure*	Thomas Hardy

JUPITER	"The Gold Bug"	Edgar Allan Poe
KADDISH	*The Ministry of Special Cases*	Nathan Englander
KAFKA	*Kafka on the Shore*	Haruki Murakami
LAIRD	*In the Gloaming*	Alice Elliot Dark
LEMUEL	*Gulliver's Travels*	Jonathan Swift
LOCH	*The Golden Apples*	Eudora Welty
MACON	*Song of Solomon*	Toni Morrison
	The Accidental Tourist	Anne Tyler
MAGNUS	*The Accidental*	Ali Smith
MARIUS	*Les Misérables*	Victor Hugo
MELCHIOR	*Brideshead Revisited*	Evelyn Waugh
MILO	*Catch-22*	Joseph Heller
MINGUS	*The Fortress of Solitude*	Jonathan Lethem
MISHA	*Absurdistan*	Gary Shteyngart
ORLANDO	*Orlando*	Virginia Woolf
ORNO	*For Kings and Planets*	Ethan Canin
OSKAR	*Extremely Loud and Incredibly Close*	Jonathan Safran Foer
PHINEAS	*Phineas Finn*	Anthony Trollope
PRAXIS	*Praxis*	Fay Weldon
QUEBEC	*Bleak House*	Charles Dickens
QUILLEN	*Sea Glass*	Anita Shreve
QUINTUS	*Titus Andronicus*	William Shakespeare
RHETT	*Gone With the Wind*	Margaret Mitchell
RILEY	*The Grass Harp*	Truman Capote
RODION	*Crime and Punishment*	Fyodor Dostoevsky

ROMEO	*Romeo and Juliet*	William Shakespeare
RUFUS	*A Death in the Family*	James Agee
SAMSON	*Man Walks Into a Room*	Nicole Krauss
SANTIAGO	*The Old Man and the Sea*	Ernest Hemingway
SAWYER	*The Adventures of Tom Sawyer*	Mark Twain
SEBASTIAN	*Brideshead Revisited*	Evelyn Waugh
SENECA	*Babbitt*	Sinclair Lewis
SEPTIMUS	*The Mystery of Edwin Drood*	Charles Dickens
SILAS	*Silas Marner*	George Eliot
TAFT	*End Zone*	Don DeLillo
TRISTAN	*Tristan*	Gottfried von Strassburg
TRISTRAM	*Tristram Shandy*	Laurence Sterne
UTAH	*Under Milkwood*	Dylan Thomas
VALENTINO	*What Is the What*	Dave Eggers
VIVALDO	*Another Country*	James Baldwin
WOLF	*The Sea Wolf*	Jack London
YANCEY	*Cimarron*	Edna Ferber
ZOOEY	*Franny and Zooey*	J. D. Salinger

And don't forget two of the coolest literary names of all:

FABLE

STORY

peyton

ATHLETE NAMES

Most of the legendary stars of sports history have regular guy names like Joe and Jimmy and Michael and Mickey (not to mention Billie Jean), but some of the newer luminaries—as well as the surnames of classic athletes—offer options that go beyond the perimeters of that limited playing field:

ADALIUS	AUSTIN
AGASSI	BECKER
AHMAN	BECKHAM
ALCOTT	BJORN
ALI	BO
ALTHEA	BORIS
AMARE	BRADMAN
ARJAN	BRADY
ARMSTRONG	BRANCH
ARROYO	BRETT
ASANTE	BRONSON
ASHE	BROOKS

CAL	FRAZIER
CAMBY	GABRIELLA
CAREW	GAINES
CARMELO	GARFIELD
CATT	GARVEY
CHIPPER	GEHRIG
CLEMENS	GERAINT
CLEMENTE	GILES
COE	GRIFFEY
COLT	HANK
COOPER	HOGAN
CORBETT	HUNTER
DARKO	ISIAH
DEION	IVAN
DELTHA	JACKSON
DEMPSEY	JORDAN
DEXTER	JOSS
DMITRI	KAREEM
DUBLIN	KATARINA
EARLY	KENYON
EMBRY	KNUTE
EMMETT	KOBE
EVANDER	LANDRY
EVERT	LAVER
EVONNE	LeBRON
EWING	LENNOX
FALDO	LITO
FISK	LLEYTON

LONDON	REESE
LUTE	RIGBY
LUTHER	RIO
MAGIC	RYNE
MALONE	SABO
MANNING	SARAZEN
MARBLE	SEBASTIAN
MARINO	SERENA
MARIS	SHAQUILLE
MARQUIS	STIRLING
MARTINA	TAI
McENROE	TAKEO
MELKY	TAMECKA
MIA	THIERRY
MING	THORPE
MONTANA	THURMAN
MOSS	TIGER
MUTU	TINKER
NEVILLE	TRIS
NOLAN	TROY
ORLANDO	TUNNEY
PALMER	TYSON
PAYTON	VENTURA
PEERLESS	VENUS
PELÉ	VIDA
PEYTON	VIJAY
PICABO	WEST
PLAXICO	WILKO
PRIEST	ZELMO

pre-cool
cool

OLD NAMES

octavia

ANCIENT NAMES

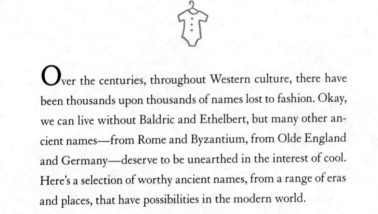

Over the centuries, throughout Western culture, there have been thousands upon thousands of names lost to fashion. Okay, we can live without Baldric and Ethelbert, but many other ancient names—from Rome and Byzantium, from Olde England and Germany—deserve to be unearthed in the interest of cool. Here's a selection of worthy ancient names, from a range of eras and places, that have possibilities in the modern world.

girls

ABELIA	ATARAH
AELIANA	ATHALIA
ALBIA	AURELIA
AMICA	AVITA
ANNIA	BASILIA
APHRA	BEATA
AQUILIA	CALVINA
ARGENTIA	CAMPANA
ARRIA	CANDIDA

CASSIA	HONORIA
CLEMENCIA	HORATIA
COLUMBA	ISOLDE
CONSTANTINA	JENNET
CRISPINA	JOLECIA
CYRA	JONET
DAMARIS	JUNIA
DAMIANE	JUNO
DECIMA	JUSTINA
DELICIA	LAELIA
DEULCIA	LAURENTIA
DOMINICA	LIVIA
DRUSILLA	LUCIA
ELIZABELLA	LUCILLA
ELLOT	LUCRETIA
FABIA	MAHALA
FANNIA	MARABLE
FAUSTA	MARCIANA
FAUSTINA	MARILLA
FELICIA	MAXIMA
FLAVIA	MELISENT
FLORENTINA	MERAUDE
FORTUNATA	MERIALL
GAIA	MILA
GALLA	MINERVA
GAYNOR	MUCIA
GWENORE	NERILLA
HILARIA	NICASIA

OCTAVIA

PACCIA

PALATINA

PERPETUA

PERSIS

PHILLIDA

PLACIDIA

PRIMA/PRIMULA

QUINTIA/QUINTINA

RUFINA

SABINA

SEPTIMA

SERGIA

SEVERINA

SILVIA

SINETTA

TACIBA

TANAQUIL

TAURIA

TERTIA

TITIANA

TULLIA

TURIA

URBANA

VALENTINA

VALERIA

VARINIA

VERINA

VIVIANA

ZELINA

boys

AENEAS

AMADEUS

ANDREAS

ANTONIUS

APOLLOS

ATTICUS

AUGUSTUS

AURELIUS

CAESAR

CAIUS

CASSIUS

CATO

CICERO

CLAUDIUS

CORNELIUS

COSMO

CYRUS

DECIMUS

DEMETRIUS

FELIX

FLAVIUS

GAIUS

HORATIO

JUSTUS

LAZARUS	REMUS
LUCIUS	ROMANUS
MAGNUS	ROMULUS
MARCELLUS	RUFUS
MARCUS	SENECA
MARIUS	SEPTIMUS
MAXIMUS	SEVERUS
NAZARES	STEPHANUS
NERO	TARQUIN
OCTAVIUS	THEON
PHILO	TIBERIUS
PRIMUS	TITUS
QUINTUS	URBAN

COOLEST
ANCIENT NAME
• • •
Atticus

boaz

HOLY NAMES

Some of the coolest names we've come across in researching this book were found in the least likely sources: the Bible and guides to the saints. If you want to know the provenance of the names that follow—who Lydia was in the Bible, for instance, or what made St. Swithun so special—you're going to have to consult a source that deals with that sort of hard information. We're just here to tell you that these names are cool . . . and won't make the priest blanch at the baptismal font.

girls

ADAH	AUDREY
ADALIA	AZUBAH
AGATHA	BATHSHEBA/SHEBA
AGNES	BEATRICE
ALICE	BERNADETTE
ANASTASIA	BETHIA
APOLLONIA	BIBIANA
AQUILINA	CEARA

CECILIA	MAHALAH
CLARE	MARA
CLAUDIA	MATILDA
DAMARIS	MELANIA
DARIA	MICHAL
DEBORAH	MIRIAM
DELILAH	MORGANA
DELPHINA	MORIAH
DINAH	NATALIA
EMILIANA	PERSIS
ESTHER	PHOEBE
EVE	PRISCILLA
FABIOLA	RIONA
FAITH	SALOME
FELICITY	SANCHIA
GEMMA	SAPPHIRA
GERMAINE	SARAI
HADASSAH	SELAH
HELENA	SERAPHINA
ISABEL	SHUA
JAEL	TABITHA
JEMIMA	TALITHA
JERUSHA	TAMAR
KETURAH	TATIANA
KEZIAH	THEA
LILITH	URSULA
LUCY	VERONICA
LYDIA	ZILLAH

boys

ABEL	BRENDAN
ABIJAH	BRICE
ABNER	BROGAN
ABRAHAM	BRUNO
ABSALOM	CALEB
ADLAI	CASSIAN
ADRIAN	CLEMENT
ALBAN	CLETE
AMBROSE	CONALL
AMOS	CONAN
ANSELM	CRISPIN
ASA	CYPRIAN
ASHER	CYRIAC
AUBREY	DAMIAN
AUGUSTINE	DECLAN
AZARIAH	DOMINIC
BARAK	DONAN
BARNABAS	DUNSTAN
BARTHOLOMEW	ELEAZAR
BARUCH	ELIAS
BARZILLAI	ELIJAH
BASIL	ELISHA
BECAN	EPHRAIM
BENEDICT	ERASMUS
BENNO	ESAU
BLASE	EZEKIEL
BOAZ	EZRA

FABIAN	JUBAL
FELIX	JUDAH
FINNIAN	JUDE
FRANCIS	JULIAN
GABRIEL	JUSTIN
GERMAIN	JUSTUS
GERVASE	KENELM
GIDEON	KILLIAN
GILES	LAZARUS
HIRAM	LEMUEL
HOSEA	LEO
HUGH	LEVI
ISAAC	LINUS
ISAIAH	LUCIAN
ISHMAEL	LUCIUS
ISIDORE	LUKE
IVO	MALACHI
JABEZ	MATTHIAS
JADON	MICAH
JAPHETH	MOAB
JARED	MOSES
JAVAN	NOE
JEDIDIAH	OBADIAH
JEHU	OLIVER
JETHRO	OMAR
JOAB	PHINEAS
JOACHIM	PIRAN
JOSIAH	QUENTIN

RAPHAEL	SOLOMON
REMI	SWITHUN
REUBEN	THADDEUS
REUEL	TIARNAN
ROMAN	TITUS
RUPERT	TOBIAH
SAMSON	URBAN
SAUL	VITAL
SEBASTIAN	ZACHARIAS
SETH	ZEBEDEE
SIMEON	ZEBEDIAH
SIMON	ZEDEKIAH
SIXTUS	

COOLEST
BIBLICAL NAME
• • •
Jabez

BIBLICAL PLACE NAMES

ABILENE	LYDDA
ARIEL	LYSTRA
BETHANY	MARAH
BETHEL	MORIAH
BEULAH	ONO
CANAAN	SAMARIA
CARMEL	SHAMIR
DANNAH	SHEBA
EDEN	SHILOH
ETHAM	SINAI
IDALAH	UZ
IVAH	ZAIR
JERICHO	ZEBULUN
JORDAN	ZELAH
JUDAH	ZION
KEILAH	ZORAH

obadiah

COLONIAL NAMES

Many of the names that were widely used during colonial times have fallen out of favor for long enough now to sound fresh and even cool again. If you like historic names but want to move beyond the Victorian and biblical choices we've heard so much of in recent years, consider these names culled from Revolutionary War rolls and eighteenth-century town histories. The only caveat: The choices are much wider and more appealing for boys than for girls.

girls

ABITHA	DORCAS	HESTER
AMITY	ELECTA	KETURAH
APHRA	EMELINE	KEZIAH
AURINDA	ESTER	LYDIA
AZUBA	FANNY	MAHALA
CHARITY	HECUBA	MERCY
COMFORT	HENRIETTA	MODESTY
CORNELIA	HEPZIBAH	PATIENCE

PHILA	ARCHIBALD	EZEKIEL
PHOEBE	ASA	GIDEON
PRIMROSE	ASAHEL	HANNIBAL
PRUDENCE	AZARIAH	HEZEKIAH
REBEKAH	BALTHASAR	HIRAM
REMEMBER	BARNABAS	HOMER
ROSANNA	BARTHOLOMEW	HORATIO
SELAH	BAZEL	HOSEA
SUSANNA	BENAJAH	INCREASE
TABITHA	CLEMENT	ISAAC
TEMPERANCE	COMFORT	ISAIAH
THEODOSIA	CONSTANT	ISHAM
VERITY	COTTON	ISRAEL
	CYRUS	JARED
boys	EBENEZER	JEDIDIAH
ABIEL	ELEAZAR	JEHU
ABIJAH	ELI	JEREMIAH
ABIMAEL	ELIAB	JETHRO
ABNER	ELIAKIM	JONAS
ABRAHAM	ELIAS	JOSIAH
ABSALOM	ELIHU	JOTHAN
ADONIJAH	ELIJAH	LAZARUS
ALDEN	ELIPHALET	LEMUEL
AMIAS/AMYAS	ELISHA	LEVI
AMIEL	EMANUEL	LINUS
AMMIRAS	EMORY	MICAJAH
AMOS	ENOCH	NEHEMIAH
AMZI	EXPERIENCE	OBADIAH

PHILO	SAMPSON	ZACHARIAH
PHILOMON	SETH	ZADOCK
PHINEAS	SOLOMON	ZEBULON
PROSPERITY	THADDEUS	ZEPHANIAH
REASON	THEOPHILUS	ZOPHAR
RUFUS	TRUTH	
SALMON	ZACCHEUS	

COOLEST
VIRTUE NAME
• • •
Amity

mel

GEEZER NAMES FOR GIRLS

Blame it on Sidney. This name, which conjures up images of thick glasses, a snowfall of dandruff on shoulders, and plaid polyester pants pulled up to the sternum, sounds—strangely enough—nothing less than charming, nothing short of cool when applied to a little girl. And so too can the other geezer names here. Caution: Most of these names should not be bestowed on a boy. The world is not yet ready for another generation of male Seymours and Sheldons—although keep in mind that among the hottest boys' names in the UK now are Harvey and Leon.

ARTHUR	FLOYD
BARRY	GARY
BERT	HOWARD
CHAUNCEY	IRA
CLARENCE	JAY
CYRIL	JULES
ERNEST	LAWRENCE
ERROL	LESTER

LLOYD	REGGIE
LYLE	ROSCOE
MARLON	ROY
MARSHALL	RUDY
MARTIN	SETH
MARVIN	SEYMOUR
MAURY	SHELDON
MEL	SIDNEY
MILTON	SILAS
MONROE	SINCLAIR
MORLEY	STANLEY
MORRIS	STUART
MURRAY	VERNON
NEAL	VINCENT
NORRIS	VIRGIL
PERCY	WALLACE
PERRY	WENDELL
RANDOLPH	ZEKE

matilda

OLD-LADY COOL

If you like that fusty old feel but you're not ready to go all the way to Murray for your daughter, you might want to consider the old-lady names here, cool by virtue of their very disdain for fashion.

ADA	CELIA	EUDORA
ADELAIDE	CLARA	EUGENIA
ADELIA	CONSTANCE	EVELYN
ADELINE	CORA	FAY
AGATHA	CORDELIA	FLORA
AGNES	CORNELIA	FLORENCE
ALBERTA	DORA	FRANCES
ALMA	DOROTHEA	FREDERICA
ANASTASIA	EDITH	GERALDINE
ANTONIA	ELSA	HARRIET
AUGUSTA	ELSIE	HAZEL
BEATRICE	ESTHER	HELEN
BLANCHE	ETTA	HENRIETTA

HERMIONE	MABEL	PEARL
IDA	MAMIE	PENELOPE
IMOGEN	MARTHA	PRISCILLA
IRIS	MATILDA	PRUDENCE
IVY	MAUDE	RUTH
JOSEPHINE	MAY	THEODORA
KAY	MILLICENT	URSULA
LAVINIA	MINERVA	VERA
LEONORA	MIRIAM	VIOLA
LETITIA	MURIEL	VIVIAN
LUCASTA	MYRTLE	WILHELMINA
LUCINDA	OLIVE	WINIFRED
LUCRETIA	OPAL	ZENOBIA

**COOLEST
NUT NAME**

• • •

Hazel

elmer

NAMES NO ONE MAY BE COOL ENOUGH FOR

You have to be pretty damn cool to name your kid Elmer, cool in that I-like-it-and-I-don't-care-what-the-world-thinks kind of way. Except you're not the one who's going to have to deal with having the name Elmer when you play Little League. You're not the one who's going to have to introduce yourself as Elmer to girls at parties. In fact, if you think it's so cool, maybe you should change your own name to Elmer rather than laying it on a poor little kid.

The point: While we can appreciate the contrarian cool inherent in these clunky names, we fear that few children at this point in time are cool enough actually to live with them.

girls

BERTHA	EDNA
BEULAH	ELBERTA
BRUNHILDA	ERNESTINE
DORIS	ETHEL

EUNICE	EDGAR
FULVIA	EGBERT
GAY	ELMER
GERTRUDE	GOMER
GRISELDA	HANSEL
HELGA	HERMAN
HERMIA	HUBERT
HESTER	HYMAN/HYMIE
HILDEGARDE	IRVING
HORTENSE	MAURICE
IRMA	MELVIN
JOYCE	MERVYN
MEHITABEL	MILTON
MILDRED	MONTAGUE
MYRNA	NORBERT
PHYLLIS	OSBERT
SHIRLEY	OSWALD
VIGDIS	SEYMOUR
YETTA	SHELDON
	SHERMAN
boys	SHERWIN
ARCHIBALD	SIEGFRIED
ARNOLD	STANLEY
BERNARD	URIAH
BERTRAM	WILBUR
BURTON	WILFRED
DELBERT	WILLIS
DURWOOD	

new cool

CREATIVE NAMES

tierra

FOREIGN-WORD NAMES

For many prospective parents, the definition of a cool name is one that is unique. This taste for one-of-a-kind names is not surprising when you consider that many new moms and dads grew up with megapopular names themselves and feel that it sacrificed some of their individuality. Masses of new moms, for instance, are named Jennifer, the number one name from 1970 to 1985, and the name became so generic that there are now Jennifer support groups on the Internet and a Society for the Prevention of Parents Naming Their Children Jennifer. There were almost equal numbers of Jessicas, Amandas, Lisas, Michelles, Amys, and Heathers, not to mention all those Jeffs, Joshes, Jonathans, and Jasons.

In a larger sense, there is a general feeling of depersonalization and lack of distinctive identity in this era of ID codes and PINs, causing many parents to want to create a singular appellation for their children. And then there's the movement over the past decade or so toward increasingly unusual names, with new ethnic names, place names, surname names, and words as names jumping into the mix. The parent who wants a truly distinctive name for his or her baby has to move farther than ever away from the established roster.

One new direction—or is it two?—for the intrepid baby namer is toward foreign-word names, which combines two of today's coolest trends. We combed our own diccionarios for French, Italian, and Spanish words that could make perfectly appropriate, attractive names for your baby, but no reason to stop here. Consider words from the language of your own ethnic background, be it Czech or Chinese, and add them to the list of your personal possibilities.

FRENCH

AÉRIEN	airy
ALÉA	chance
ALIZÉ	soft cloud
ALOUETTE	lark
AMANDE	almond
AMBRETTE	almond seed
AMÉRIQUE	America
ANGE	angel
ANNEAU	ring, ringlet
ATLANTIQUE	Atlantic
BECHETTE	little spade
BICHETTE	little doe
BIJOU	jewel

BLEU	blue
BONTÉ	goodness, bounty
BRIN	sprig
CADEAU	gift
CANDIDE	open, frank
CHATON	kitten
DEJA	already
DELÀ	beyond
DÉLICE	delight
DIMANCHE	Sunday
DORÉ	gilded
ELLE	she
FABRIQUE	fabric
FLAMBEAU	flame, candle
FLEUR	flower
FLEURETTE	little flower
FRAISE	strawberry
GALETTE	flat cake
ICI	here
JADIS	in olden times
JAMAIS	never
JANVIER	January
JETON	marker, token
JOLIE	pretty
JUMELLE	twin
LARIGOT	ancient flute
LEXIQUE	lexicon, vocabulary
LIVRET	little book

LORIOT	oriole
LUMIÈRE	light
LUNE	moon
MAI	May
MAISON	house
MARDI	Tuesday
MARÉE	tide
MARGAY	tiger cat
MARRON	chestnut
MAUVE	seagull
MELILOT	sweet clover
MERISE	wild cherry
MIRABELLE	yellow plum
MOINEAU	sparrow
MUSIQUE	music
NEIGE	snow
NICHÉE	nest of young birds
PARC	park
PLAIRE	to please
POMME	apple
REINE	queen
RIVAGE	shore
ROCHE	rock
ROUX	reddish brown
RUBAN	ribbon
SAISON	season
SAMEDI	Saturday
SANSONNET	starling

SATINÉ	satiny
SAVARIN	round cake
SÉJOUR	sojourn
SEMAINE	week
SOLEIL	sun
SOMMET	summit
SONGE	dream
TERRE	earth
TULIPE	tulip
VELOUTÉ	velvety
VICTOIRE	victory
VRAI	true
VRILLE	tendril

ITALIAN

ADAGIO	slowly, gently
AIO	tutor, teacher
ALBA	dawn
ALEA	chance, risk
ALITO	breath, light breeze
ALLEGRO	cheerful, merry
ALZATA	rising up, elevation
ANNATA	year's time
AQUILA	eagle
ARDESIA	slate
ARIA	air
AURETTA	gentle breeze

AURORA	dawn
BAIA	bay
BALIA	power, authority, children's nurse
BALZO	leap
BELLEZZA	beautiful woman
BENNATO	wellborn, generous
BIANCO	white
BLU	blue
BRIO	spirit, animation
CADENZA	cadence
CALA	cove, bay
CALIA	gold dust
CALLAIA	passage
CANNA	cane, reed
CAREZZA	caress
CIELO	sky
COLOMBA	dove
CORO	chorus
DANZA	dance, ball
DELFINO	dolphin
DESINATA	feast
DONNINA	good woman, clever girl
DOVIZIA	wealth, abundance
DUNA	dune
ELETTA	choice, elite
ELLERA	ivy
ELLISSE	ellipse

FABBRO	inventor
FARO	lighthouse
FE	faith
FIAMMA	flame
FIERO	proud
FIORE	flower
FRANGIA	fringe
GELSO	mulberry
GEMELLA	twin sister
GEMMA	jewel
GIADA	jade
GIOVANETTA	young girl
GRAZIA	grace
LAURO	laurel tree
LAVANDA	lavender
LILLA	lilac
LILLIALE	lilylike, white as a lily
LINDEZZA	neatness
LUNA	moon
MAGGIO	May
MANO	hand
MARENA	morello cherry
MARRONE	maroon, chestnut
MASSIMO	maximum, supreme
MATITA	pencil
MATTOLINA	wood lark
MIRA	aim
MIRANDO	wonderful

MORGANA	mirage
NERO	black
NEVATA	snowfall
NEVE	snow
OLANDA	Holland
OMBRA	shadow
ONDA	wave
ORA	hour
PASQUA	Easter
PATRIA	native land
PERLA	pearl
PRIMA	first
RIVA	seashore
RIVO	stream, brook
ROANO	roan horse
SABBIA	sand
SALITA	ascent
SCALA	stairs
SERENELLA	lilac
STELLINA	little star
TAMIA	small squirrel
TERRA	earth
TRINA	lace
VALENTIA	skill, cleverness, bravery
VALLETTA	little valley
VENTURA	destiny, fate
VERO	truth
VIA	way, street

VIOLETTA	violet
VITA	life
ZANA	basket, cradle
ZIA	aunt
ZINGARO	gypsy
ZIO	uncle

SPANISH

ALA	wing
ALBA	dawn
ALEGRÍA	gaiety
ALETA	wing
ALONDRA	lark
ALZA	rise
AMAPOLA	poppy
ARO	ring, hoop
AURORA	dawn
AVELLANA	hazelnut
BAHÍA	bay
BAYA	berry
BLANCA	white
BRÍO	energy
CADENA	chain
CALA	cove
CANELA	cinnamon
CARICIA	caress
CEDRO	cedar

CHARRA	horsewoman
CIELO	sky
COLINA	hill
CONCHA	shell
CORTESÍA	courtesy
CRUZ	cross
DÍA	day
ESTRELLA	star
FLOR	flower
GALÁN	romantic hero
GALAXIA	galaxy
GANA	wish, desire
GARBO	poise
GAVIOTA	seagull
INDIO	Indian
ISLA	island
JABÓN	soap
JACA	pony
JACINTO	hyacinth
JAZMÍN	jasmine
JOYA	jewel
JÚBILO	joy
LAGO	lake
LEAL	loyal
LIENZO	linen
LOA	praise
LONA	canvas
LUNA	moon
LUZ	light

MAJO	nice
MAÑA	skill
MAREA	tide
MATIZ	shade, nuance
MEJILLA	cheek
MIRA	sight
OLA	wave
ORILLA	shore
PALOMA	pigeon, dove
PERLA	pearl
QUINTA	villa
REINA	queen
RENO	reindeer
RUBÍ	ruby
SABIO	wise
SEMILLA	seed
TALLA	carving
TÍA	aunt
TIERRA	country
TIZA	chalk
TRAZA	appearance
VAJILLA	dishes
VALETA	weather vane
VEGA	fertile plain
VELADA	evening
VENTURA	happiness, luck
VIDA	life
ZAFIRO	sapphire

zen

SPIRITUAL NAMES

The post-9/11 world is more attuned to spirituality than ever. Names that suggest qualities we'd all like our children to aspire to fit our new definition of cool. While they seem as if they can work for both genders, most have been veering toward the feminine side. A few, such as Trinity, Destiny, Sky, and Genesis, are already staples on the girls' popularity lists. Many of the others might be fresh suggestions for either a boy or a girl, or for a middle name if too extreme for a first name.

ANGEL	DHARMA
ANSWER	DIVINITY
ARCADIA	DREAM
BLISS	EASTER
BODHI	EDEN
CHARITY	ETHEREAL
CHRISTMAS	EVER
DESTINY	FAITH
DEVA	FORTUNE

GENESIS	NEVAEH
GRACE	PAX
HALCYON	PAZ
HARMONY	PEACE
HEAVEN	PRAISE
INFINITY	PROMISE
JUSTICE	PRUDENCE
KISMET	SERENITY
LIGHT	SKY
LOURDES	SPIRIT
MADONNA	TAROT
MERCY	TRINITY
MESSIAH	TRUE
MIRACLE	TRUST
MOON	ZEN
MYSTERY	ZION

**COOLEST
SPICE NAME**

• • •

Clove

mauve

Amber started it, and then Rose drove the point home. Now color names have exploded beyond these once cool favorites to include hues from the obvious—Violet and Scarlet—to the most exotic, from Azure to Zinc. Blue has become almost as popular a middle name as Rose: Cher was one of the first to use it for her son Elijah, and now we have Jackson Blue (Maria Bello), Molly Blue (Veronica Webb), Rosanna Arquette's Zoe Blue, John Travolta & Kelly Preston's gallicized Ella Bleu, and the rocker Dave (U2) Evans's daughter, Blue Angel. Other colorful starbabies include Jennifer Garner & Ben Affleck's daughter Violet, Sting's Fuschia (who is called Kate), Tobey Maguire's Ruby, and a couple of Scarlet/Scarletts. The full spectrum:

ALIZARIN	AZURE/AZURA
AMETHYST	BEIGE
AQUA	BRICK
ASH	BROWN
AUBURN	BUFF

BURGUNDY	JET
CERISE	LAVENDER
CERULEAN	LILAC
CHAMOIS (pronounced	MAGENTA
shammy)	MAHOGANY
CHERRY	MAIZE
CITRON	MARIGOLD
CLARET	MAUVE
COCOA	MOSS
CORDOVAN	OLIVE
CRIMSON	PINK
CYAN	POPPY
DOVE	RAVEN
EBONY	RED
ECRU	ROAN
EMERALD	ROSE
FUCHSIA	RUBY
GINGER	RUSSET
GRANITE	SAPPHIRE
GRAY/GREY	SCARLET
GREEN	SIENNA
GREIGE	SILVER
HAZEL	SLATE
HENNA	STEEL
HYACINTH	STERLING
INDIGO	TAWNY
IVORY	TEAL
JADE	TITIAN

TOPAZ	VIOLET
TURQUOISE	VIRIDIAN
UMBER	XANTHENE
VERMILION	ZINC

cadence

MUSICAL NAMES

If it's true that music "has charms to soothe a savage breast" and is "the food of love," then it stands to reason that the words used to describe music would be charming and soothing, lyrical, rhythmic, and rousing, Some of them could even make for melodious baby names.

ADAGIO	CANARY	FIFE
ALLEGRO	CANTATA	FLAMENCO
ALTO	CAPPELLA	GIG
ARABESQUE	CAPRICE	HARMONY
ARIA	CARILLON	HARP
BANJO	CELESTE	JAZZ
BELL	CELLO	LARK
BRIO	CHANSON	LUTE
CADENCE	CLARION	LYRE
CADENZA	DIVA	LYRIC
CALLIOPE	DULCIMER	MADRIGAL
CALYPSO	ETUDE	MALAGUEÑA

MANDOLIN	REED	SONATINA
MARIMBA	RHAPSODY	SYMPHONY
MELODY	RHYTHM	TANGO
MINUET	ROCK	TEMPO
OPERA	SERAPHINE	TIMPANI
PIPER	SERENADE	TOCCATA
RAGA	SONATA	VIOLA

**COOLEST
WINTER NAME**

• • •

Snow

aries

SPACE NAMES

There are cool celebrity star names like Uma and Bono, and then there are the even more extreme astronomical star and constellation names, which might appeal to parents looking for something unique and celestial—in other words, a heavenly name. Some stellar ideas:

ADHARA	AURORA
ALCYONE	AZHA
ALIOTH	BELLATRIX
ALTAIR	CAPELLA
ALULA	CASSIOPEIA
ALYA	CHARA
ANDROMEDA	ELECTRA
ARIES	IZAR
ASCELLA	JUPITER
ASTRA	LIBRA
ATLAS	LUNA
ATRIA	MAIA

MARS	RIGEL
MEISSA	SABIK
MERCURY	SHAULA
METEOR	STAR
MIRA	TALITHA
NASHIRA	VEGA
NAVI	VENUS
NOVA	ZANIAH
ORION	ZOSMA

bravery

NON-NAME NAMES

In our book *Beyond Jennifer & Jason, Madison & Montana,* we included vast numbers of word names, nature names, day names, and surname names. While these names are, for the most part, undoubtedly cool, there are an uncountable number of them, beyond the scope of any one book. The only limits are your reference books, your imagination, and your taste. If you'd like to explore further in this territory on your own, we can direct you to *J & J, M & M,* as well as to our *Baby Name Bible,* your personal dictionary, field guide, and phone book. To give you an idea of some of the selections from these categories, we offer, here, a few of the most evocative:

AFTERNOON	BOGART	CHRISTMAS
ARBOR	BRAVERY	CRICKET
BAY	CABOT	CURRY
BEECH	CADENCE	DECEMBER
BELL	CAMEO	DOE
BIRCH	CEDAR	DOVE

DREAM	JET	PINE
DUNE	JONQUIL	PRAIRIE
EARLY	JUNIPER	QUARRY
EASTER	KEATON	QUINTESSENCE
ECHO	LANE	RANGER
EDISON	LARK	SALMON
FABLE	LINCOLN	SEASON
FIELD	MADIGAN	SNOW
FREE	MAIZE	STORY
FROST	MONDAY	TATE
GLADE	MOON	TOPAZ
GROVE	NAVY	TUESDAY
HAVEN	NORTH	TRUTH
HOLIDAY	NOVEMBER	WREN
ISLE	PIKE	

COOLEST
WATER NAME

• • •

Bay

samanda

INVENTED NAMES

Some parents attempt to come up with a cool name by inventing one of their own. They may alter a too-ordinary name, vary a spelling or a pronunciation, or cobble together several euphonic but previously unrelated syllables. But the result, too often, is far from cool. An uncool name is rarely improved by starting it with a Z instead of a J, or by adding a "sha" or a "ton" to the end.

We have heard of a few such experimentations that may hold some appeal—a short list follows. But mostly, we implore you, with all the other cool names out there, don't try this at home.

BRAYDEN	CHRISTIA
BRIENNA	DAVIN
BROGAN	GARREN
BRYSON	GREYSON
CALTON	JAXON
CASON	JAYA
CHASEN	KALLIN

KIERRA	TADEN
KIRANDA	TALLEY
KYLER	TAYLA
PAYDEN	TEAGAN
SAMANDA	TEVIN
SAYLOR	TREYTON
TACY	ZAILEY

(an)drea

STREAMLINED NAMES

Another approach to creative naming, this one as old as ElizaBETH and EuGENE, is to drop the first syllable or syllables, or even an initial letter of a name. These days, for instance, Drew and Ward are cooler than Andy or Ed. Here are some other possibilities but, as with most recipes, feel free to improvise.

(H)ARLEY	**(Ca)MILLA**
(Ga)BRIELLA	**(Ara)MINTA**
(Pris)CILLA	**(Cor)NELIA**
(Mal)COLM	**(Va)NESSA**
(An)DREA	**(Vero)NICA**
(An)JELICA	**(Je)REMY**
(Eze)KIEL	**(Ad)RIAN**
(O)LIVIA	**(Gab)RIELLA**
(A)LONZO	**(Ana)STASIA**
(A)MANDA	**(Mon)TANA**
(A)MELIA	**(Oc)TAVIA**

(Ma)TILDA	(Ale)XANDER
(Syl)VIA	(Ale)XANDRA
(Ir)VING	(A)ZIZA

NAME.DOT.NAME

Accents and hyphens have been around for a long time, used mainly in French names to indicate pronunciation or link a double name: think Renée-Thérèse. Then accents and hyphens started straying to places they didn't technically belong, all in the service of making names more interesting, more unusual, cooler (singer/actress Brandy called her daugher Sy'rai). Now the new way to add punctuation interest to a name is with the—what else?—dot, as in the ubiquitous dot.com. Singer India.arie is perhaps the best-known example of this, but hip-hoppers Will.i.am and apl.de.ap of Black Eyed Peas have joined in, transforming the practice from a one-person aberration to a trend.

bebop

TOO-COOL NAMES

Maybe you can't be too rich or too thin, but if you're a name, it just may be possible to be too cool. What makes a name too cool? Trying so hard that coolness is its main—and maybe its only—merit. Being so aggressively hip that poor little Bebop will bend under the expectations of grooviness created by his name. Sure, there are kids named Babe or Brawny who grow into their names' images, but you're asking a lot of a child who, let's face it, is just as likely to have crooked teeth and a shyness issue as a perfect body.

While the line of what constitutes a too-cool name seems to get redrawn every day, these choices will probably be on the wrong side of it for a long time to come:

BABE	BUSTER
BANJO	CABERNET
BEBOP	CALIFORNIA
BLUEBELL	CONGO
BUCK	COUGAR

COUNT	RACER
COUNTESS	RAMBO
CROCKETT	REBEL
CRUISE	REBOP
DUKE	REIGNBOW
FREE	ROCKET
GODDESS	ROGUE
GYPSY	SATCHEL
HEATHCLIFF	SCORPIO
KOOL	SHOOTER
LETHAL	SINBAD
LUCKY	SPECK
MAJESTY	SUGAR
MAVERICK	TALON
MESSIAH	TARZAN
PIRATE	TIGER
PLUTO	VICE
PORSCHE	VULCAN
POWER	WHIZDOM
PRINCE	WILD
PRINCESS	ZEPPELIN

Index

about the authors

Pamela Redmond Satran, who has been collaborating with Linda Rosenkrantz on baby name books for more than twenty years, is also the author of five novels: *Suburbanistas, Younger, Babes in Captivity, The Man I Should Have Married,* and *The Home for Wayward Supermodels.* A contributing editor for *Parenting* magazine, she cowrites the popular Glamour List column for *Glamour* magazine and writes frequently for such publications as *The New York Times, Bon Appétit, Self,* and *The Huffington Post.* Pam lives with her husband and three children—daughter, Rory, and sons, Joe and Owen—near New York City. You can visit her Web site at www.pamelaredmondsatran.com.

Linda Rosenkrantz is the author of several nonname books, including *Telegram! Modern History As Told Through More Than 400 Witty, Poignant, and Revealing Telegrams* and the memoir *My Life as a List: 207 Things About My (Bronx) Childhood,* and is coauthor (with her husband, Christopher Finch) of *Gone Hollywood* and *Sotheby's Guide to Animation Art.* In addition to contributing articles to numerous magazines, she writes a nationally syndicated column on collectibles. She lives in Los Angeles and named her daughter Chloe.

Please visit their baby name Web site at www.coolnamer.com.

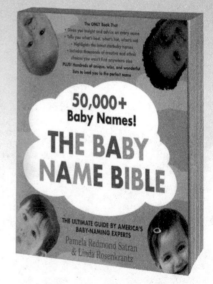
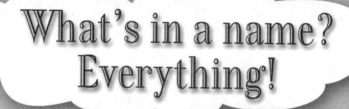